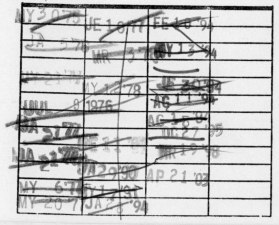

THE FREE SCHOOL

THE
FREE SCHOOL

W. Kenneth Richmond

Methuen & Co Ltd
11 New Fetter Lane, London EC4

First published 1973 by Methuen & Co. Ltd
11 New Fetter Lane, London EC4
© 1973 by W. Kenneth Richmond
Printed in Great Britain by
Butler & Tanner Ltd, Frome and London

SBN 416 75920 3
416 75930 0 paperback

Distributed in the USA by
HARPER & ROW PUBLISHERS INC.
BARNES & NOBLE IMPORT DIVISION

CONTENTS

ACKNOWLEDGEMENTS

The author and publishers wish to thank the following for permission to reproduce material from the publications listed below.

Calder & Boyers Ltd and Doubleday & Company Inc. for *Deschooling Society* by Ivan Illich; City Lights Publishers for *Planet News 1961–67* by Allen Ginsberg; Codsall Comprehensive School for appendix material; Collier–Macmillan Ltd for *The Adolescent Society* by J. S. Coleman; Coombe Lodge for *The Use of Resources* report; the Critical Quarterly Society for *Black Papers on Education* edited by C. B. Cox and A. E. Dyson; *Den Frie Laere Skole* for the August 1966 issue; Evans Brothers Ltd for the *1970 World Year Book of Education* edited by Joseph A. Lauwerys and David G. Scanlon; Faber & Faber Ltd for *Education and Modernization* by M. D. Shipman, *Young People and Society* by Ted Tapper; Faber & Faber Ltd and Doubleday & Company Inc. for *The Making of a Counter Culture* by Theodore Roszak; the *Guardian* and John Hall for the 29 September 1971 issue; Hamish Hamilton Ltd and Houghton Mifflin Inc. for *The Affluent Society* by J. K. Galbraith; Harvard University Press for *General Education in a Free Society*, a report of the Harvard Committee; Her Majesty's Stationery Office for *Half Our Future*, a report on education (1963); Home Base School for appendix material; the Institute of Economic Affairs for *Education and the State* by E. G. West; Ivan Illich for an unpublished paper; John Adams High School for appendix material; Longman Group Ltd for *Linking*

Home and School edited by M. Craft, J. Raynor and L. Cohen;
MacGibbon & Kee Ltd for *The Concept of Popular Education* by
Harold Silver; Thomas Nelson & Sons Ltd for *The Rise of the
Public Schools* by T. W. Bamford; the *New York Saturday Review*
and Ivan Illich for the 19 June 1971 issue; the Oldbourne Press for
Comprehensive Schools in Action by R. Cole; the Parkway Program
and the Al Paul Lefton Advertising Agency for the Parkway
Program advertisement; Penguin Books Ltd and Everett Reimer
for *School is Dead* by Everett Reimer; Penguin Books Ltd for
Spare the Child by W. D. Wills, *Resources for Learning* by L. C.
Taylor; *Phi Delta Kappan* for the May 1971 issue; Theodore
Roszak for 'Education contra naturam' in *High School* edited by
R. Gross and P. Osterman; Routledge and Kegan Paul Ltd for
Political Education in a Democracy by H. Entwistle, *The Logic of
Education* by P. H. Hirst and R. S. Peters, *Education and the
Working Class* by Brian Jackson and Dennis Marsden, *Primary
School Design* by Malcolm Seaborne; Routledge and Kegan Paul
and Beacon Press for *One-Dimensional Man* by Herbert Marcuse;
the School Without Walls for appendix material; Wiley & Sons
Inc. for *The Sociology of Teaching* by Willard Waller.

Section 1

A TIME TO RECANT

A TIME TO RECANT

1 The absolute paradox

Talk of deschooling, free schooling – or should it be re-schooling?
– is suddenly *à la mode*. Loose talk, mostly. It flourishes in unlikely places, nowhere more so than in the trendier colleges and
universities. Academics, the kind who take fright at the first
murmurings of Student Power, spice their lectures – it makes a
change – with learned chat about the sociological implications of
Consciousness III-and-All-That. Graduates whose main ambition
in life is to secure a comfortable, well-paid job in the educational
services quote the latest utterances of Illich as reverentially as if
they were Holy Writ. *School is Dead* becomes a prescribed text for
courses of teacher training. In each case, the underlying assumption
in this sportive discourse is that it is not to be taken seriously.
To affect a bogus radicalism suits the mood of the moment.

In this doublethink situation an author who takes it upon himself to act as a go-between is certain to come under fire from both
sides, from the *avant-garde* who will blame him for being over-
timid and apologetic as well as from the traditionalists who will
take umbrage at many of the things he has to say. The former
would prefer a more militant, anti-establishment approach,
tauter arguments: the latter will deplore any suggestion which
looks like rocking the boat.

If the viewpoint adopted in *The Free School* is to be taken seriously, and if he is to avoid future shock, the reader is asked to come to terms with four ideas at the outset. The first is taken from an essay by Theodore Roszak, author of *The Making of a Counter Culture*; the second from that prince of heretics, Jean-Jacques Rousseau; the third from that gentlest of aesthetes, Herbert Read; the fourth from that tormented spirit, Sören Kierkegaard:

> Let us postulate a law: the less secure the culture, the larger the educational establishment. All of us readily recognize that a society in need of heavy policing must be in serious trouble – for the laws have surely lost their power to command respect. Similarly, a society that professionalizes and anxiously aggrandizes its educational establishment – its cultural cops – is also in serious trouble, for the culture has surely lost its capacity to command interest and involvement. The new chronic top-to-bottom state of emergency in our schools does not exist because the educational establishment is not good enough and needs repair. The crisis is that the culture is not good enough. The educational establishment, with all its compulsions, its disciplinary hang-ups, and – yes – even its constabulary forces patrolling the corridors – all this exists in the first place because of the insecurity of the culture[1].

> Our pedantic mania for instruction is always leading us to teach children the things they would learn better of their own accord[2].

> Anarchism means literally a society without an *arkhos*, that is to say, without a ruler. It does not mean a society without law and therefore it does not mean a society without order. The anarchist accepts the social contract, but he interprets the contract in a particular way which he believes to be the way most justified by reason[3].

> Officialdom is incommensurable with Christianity[4].

The educational 'heresies' expressed by this combination of views will invite dissent, even derision. The reader who thinks that criticisms of the education system can be kept apart from criticisms of society may be out of sympathy with the argument to begin with, and out of patience before the end. He does not have to agree with Roszak that we are faced with a chronic state of emergency in our schools, though he can hardly turn a blind eye to the daily reports of unruliness, violence and antisocial behaviour in the classroom. He does not have to agree that what is seen as a cultural crisis in the USA need necessarily be viewed as such in Britain though he would be well advised – when saying 'it can't happen here' – to keep his intellectual fingers crossed. Neither does he have to agree with Rousseau that teachers are no better than pedantic maniacs, though one would hope that he is not so wrong-headed as to deny that children's learning is most effective when self-directed. He should also be warned against the temptation to dismiss ideas which strike him as ridiculous or outrageous as 'anarchical', simply because they would upset the *status quo*. It is an easy defence, but not a valid one.

What the reader *is* asked to do, however – and on this the author admits of no compromise – is to come to terms with Kierkegaard's Absolute Paradox: either Christ or the Church. In short, the dilemma presented by the inner conflict between personal faith and organized religion now manifests itself as the conflict between education and schooling.

The analogy holds if only because education has become the secular substitute for religion in the modern world. As Thomas Huxley feared might happen, it has become 'an Established Church Scientific, with a hierarchical organization and a Profes-sorial Episcopate'. Universities have taken over from the cathedrals as the central institutions in an industrial society. Church over-lordship has been superseded by state control of the schools. Monastic theory and practice, originally designed for the training of clerics, still dominate our concepts of academic secondary schooling. Our ideas about what constitutes learning are condi-tioned by beliefs, values and myths which antedate the Protestant ethic itself.

Even the cult of literacy, for long the main business, if not the only one, of mass instruction, may now be seen as a proper study for the industrial archaeologist. It is easy to forget that the concept of popular education which is now taken for granted, i.e. the compulsory enrolment of all children in a special kind of institu-tion, is little more than a century old. The concept implies that education is not something which the individual can safely be allowed to get for himself but a process whereby adults master-

mind the young and tell them what they (the adults) think they
ought to know. So long as the official policy of the Church followed
St Augustine's dictum 'Faith is for the many; education is for the
few' – indeed, right up to 1870 in England and Wales – school,
as an institution, was only for those who voluntarily subjected
themselves to a life *in statu pupillari*. Previously, as we shall see in
subsequent chapters, the institutional role of the school had been
a relatively minor one. The gradual takeover of the learner's
personal development, and the wholesale expansion of the educational services which has taken place during the last fifty years
may be seen as parallelling the Christian belief that salvation can
only come by being reborn, a belief ritualized in the sacrament of
baptism; given a new twist by the Protestant reformers, notably
Comenius, it became 'If a man is to be produced it is necessary
that he be formed by education'.

This assertion is worth pondering for it represents a flat denial
of an essential tenet of Christian doctrine, namely, that man is
born a living soul. Nevertheless Comenius's words became the
keystone of educational theory and practice in an industrial society
and opened the way for techniques of prediction and control
which see nothing wrong in social and human engineering.

The Great Didactic may well be regarded as the prophetic
blueprint on which all modern national systems of education have
been modelled. As one of the first and greatest founding fathers of
educational thought in the Western world, Comenius occupies so
venerable a place in history that it comes as a distinct shock to
find his central doctrine of the universal need for the 'natural' man
to undergo a lengthy period of processing in order to achieve the
status of 'true' manhood, being challenged.

In his *Magna Didactica*, he described schools as devices 'to
teach everybody everything' and outlined a blueprint for the
assembly-line production of knowledge, which according to him
would make education cheaper and better and make growth
into full humanity possible for all. But Comenius was not only
an early efficiency expert, he was an alchemist who adopted the
technical language of his craft to describe the art of rearing
children. The alchemist sought to refine base elements by
leading their distilled spirits through twelve stages of successive
enlightenment, so that for their own and all the world's benefit

they might be transmuted into pure gold. Of course, alchemists failed no matter how often they tried, but each time their 'science' yielded new reasons for failure, and they tried again.

Pedagogy opened a new chapter in the history of *Ars Magna*. Education became the search for an alchemic process that would bring forth a new type of man, who would fit into an environment created by scientific magic. But, no matter how much each generation spent on its schools, it always turned out that the majority of people were unfit for enlightenment by this process and had to be discarded as unfit for life in a man-made world[5].

So far as the present argument is concerned it makes little difference whether we think of the modern theory and practice of education as a secular religion or as a pseudo-science. Either way, its articles of faith admit of no heresy, not least those which maintain that compulsory schooling is necessarily beneficial, the more beneficial the longer it lasts, and that the learning process is best left in the hands of certified teachers. The high priests of this latest and greatest of teaching religions can rely on the support of a respectful populace which sees the 'knowledge explosion' and the steady lengthening of school life as promoting the cause of social justice and enhancing the quality of life. Much of this busy empire-building is a form of totalitarianism that should give rise to serious disquiet.

In the United Kingdom the growing sense of dissatisfaction arises from an awareness of the less than happy state of affairs in non-selective secondary schools. What to do with the apathetic, less manageable and occasionally hostile 13 – 15-year-olds who are not enrolled for any sort of leaving-certificate course is posing increasing difficulties for those who have to cope with them, and with the raising of the school-leaving age the problem seems more than ever intractable. In England and Wales, tripartism (never more than a euphemism for what had always been a two-track system of grammar and post-primary schools) may be thought to have received its quietus with the publication of William Taylor's study *The Secondary Modern School* in 1963, yet in most areas it remains entrenched and looks like remaining so in the foreseeable future. In the meantime a number of investigations have shown that the polarization of attitudes which gives rise to a high-achieving, pro-school group on the one hand and an under-achieving, anti-school subculture is inextricably bound up with the selective function of the school organization.* This polarization, it was first thought, resulted from a conflict between working-class and middle-class life styles, but it is now realized that to explain it in this way is to oversimplify the phenomenon. Interestingly enough, although the research findings reported in the USA are broadly in line with those in Britain the problem is apparently nothing like so troublesome in France where pupils are assigned to 'long' and 'short' courses after completing 2–3 years of the *cycle d'observation* – and where classes are rigorously streamed. Fairly evidently, then, this is one problem which is *not* going to be resolved simply by reorganizing secondary schools on compre-hensive lines.

Many teachers would say that, despite all the efforts that have been made to provide interesting and attractive courses, the schools have failed in the sense that a great many pupils leave without learning much of anything that is of lasting value to them. For their part, many sociologists would say that the schools have been only too successful as agents of political socialization; 'gentling the masses', as it used to be called, has effectively confirmed the majority in the conviction of their own inferiority.

Recently the critics have become noticeably more outspoken than they were a few years ago. Few of them are quite so indignant as Edward Bond, perhaps:

> I think that universal education is one of the worst disasters that has hit Western society since the Black Death, and I think it has had a comparable effect. Once you have people at an early age in their school cage, then you've got them. I'm not against knowledge, I'm against training, against indoctrination, against regimentation. Our schools are like prisons. There's really no difference between our state prisons and our state schools. They function in the same way, to serve the same purpose. They are, in fact, training alienated slaves who will fit into our society, at least to the extent of consenting to it. We are producing zombies[6].

* Cf. D. Hargreaves, *Social Relations in a Secondary School* (RKP, 1967). C. Lacey, *Hightown Grammar* (Manchester University Press, 1970). J. Ford, *Social Class and the Comprehensive School* (RKP, 1969).

Professional opinion is veering towards a similar conclusion. L. C. Taylor, himself a distinguished headmaster, notes that secondary schooling demands far more organizational ingenuity, more controls, tighter discipline than is needed at the primary stage, the inference being that its inmates tend to be an awkward squad who are not so easily kept in check. He notes, too, how the curriculum (non-academic as well as academic) consists of 'artificial and complex matters' lacking any obvious intrinsic or instrumental value, with the result that 'The school must look after boys as if they were children and teach them as though they were adults'. At best, the collection of a few O- and A-level passes provides token rewards for the few, but this incentive cuts precious little ice with the majority, and rightly. 'If all pre-school and primary learning were blotted from our minds we should be hampered indeed; not so with secondary schooling', he concludes[7].

Again, Frank Musgrove voices the opinion that schools at present lack the power to achieve the goals they set for themselves. The remedy, he thinks, is to link them more closely with society and the 'power environment'. As things are, teachers are relatively powerless 'because they have little to offer that their pupils urgently want'. Throughout its course, indeed, Musgrove's train of thought is beset with conflicts and contradictions; his chapter on the need for greater participation and more open lines of communication is followed by one extolling the advantages of bureaucracy, a switch which leaves him and his readers in two minds. Summing up, he repeats his conviction that if schools are to attain their goals their power must somehow be increased, only to add:

But these goals may soon be pointless. Any goals for schools may soon be pointless. And there are other reasons for this than a possibly imminent cyberculture. It is not only Liam Hudson who holds the view that 'much of what passes for education in this country and the United States is a waste of everybody's time, pupils and teachers alike'. It may be an important function of schools, though it is scarcely a goal, to do precisely this – to waste the time of young people who have become socially and economically redundant. Such time wasting might be done more enjoyably, profitably and cheaply by other means.

But even in relation to educational goals which are relevant to the maintenance of our present socio-economic order, schools as we know them may be clumsy, obsolescent and unfair. These goals may be more effectively and justly pursued out of schools than in them[8].

Somewhat strangely, after reaching this verdict, Musgrove shies away from its consequences: they savour too strongly of a counter-culture which may be just around the corner in California but which is too, too remote from the practical politics of British education to be taken seriously. Yet in the advanced industrial societies, in which the tendency is for the service sectors – of which the 'information business' is by far the largest – to extend their scope, the signs are that every increase in educated man-power is accompanied by a decrease in worthwhile job opportunities. As Everett Reimer puts it:

More and more people in the wealthier countries are employed in the service sector, doing things of dubious value. Consider government and corporate bureaucrats, salesmen, advertisers, bankers, accountants, lawyers, teachers, policemen, soldiers, poll-takers, social workers, for example. There is no doubt that all these people do something that someone values, but there is little doubt that as many people hate what they do[9].

In the twilight of the Age of Faith, it is worth recalling that the peddlers of indulgences were generally thought to provide an 'essential service'. Is not the traffic in paper qualifications, to which we have all been party in our time, on a par with the mal-practices against which Luther fulminated? In New York City, it seems, you need to possess a diploma before you can be employed as a dustman. Which is absurd. The extent of the absurdity has been demonstrated in Ivar Berg's aptly-titled study *Education and Jobs: The Great Training Robbery*. The reiterated argument that an extended school life and the right examination passes prepare schoolchildren for the world of work has ceased to be convincing. According to Paul Goodman, the average job in General Motors' most automated plant requires only three weeks of training for employees who have received no education what-soever. Nor is absurdity the worst of it. What are we to say of a system which treats young people as if they were not only economically, but also socially, redundant? Surely, there must be something seriously wrong with a system which can think of nothing better to do with teenagers than to keep them marking time in an institution which in its isolation from society, must seem to many of them like a prison. Can it be that the educational services are in some respects a colossal fraud? Are the doctrines of this latest opiate of the people only preserved from falling into disrepute because they are sustained by logic-spinning and conceptual analysis as sterile as that of the medieval Schoolmen?

2 A plethora of educationists

Today's Schoolman is, of course, the educationist. Harry Truman once defined a statesman as a 'finished' politician. By the same token, educationists may be described as 'finished' teachers. With few exceptions, they began their careers inside the school classroom only to find it expedient, and more congenial, to seek their fortunes elsewhere. How many did so because they were 'failed' teachers must remain a matter for speculation. A cynic might be forgiven for thinking that if there is any truth in the jest that, 'Those who can, do; those who can't, teach', the cream of it is that those who cannot teach often become educationists. At any rate, all are 'finished' in the sense that it is highly unlikely that they will ever return to work in the schools. Though educationists, they have virtually ceased to be educators. In short, they are a parasitic breed. Their number is legion and it is growing all the time. Just how serious is the drain on the schools may be gathered from the fact that the level of competence in the teaching profession in countries like France, where educationists are thin on the ground, appears to be a good deal higher than it is in the USA, where they swarm. The unseemly haste with which educationists sever their connections with the day-to-day practice of their profession tells us something about the conditions of service and morale of that profession.

What exactly *is* an educationist? The habit of falling back on an alternative designation – 'educationalist' – indicates some uncertainty. Everyone has a fairly clear idea of what a psychologist is: at least no one dreams of calling *him* a 'psychologicalist'. He is a specialist and, unquestionably, specialization is here to stay; no one denies that specialists have their uses. But, as T. S. Eliot warned, excessive specialization may be interpreted as a sign of cultural disintegration. It is worth recalling that the rise of the Sophists (the educationists of the ancient world) heralded the break-up of the Athenian city state as a truly educative society; and that the establishment of something like a state system of schooling under Vespasian was accomplished at a time when Roman civilization was already in decline.

The charge levelled against educationists amounts to this: that they are 'doing things of dubious value', wholly unaware of it. Why 'of dubious value'? Firstly they have ceased to be educators; secondly they are kept men, so wedded to the institutions they serve that system-maintenance is part and parcel of their thinking.

They maintain an education system which treats the majority of teenagers as social rejects. From Plato to Dewey, great educators have invariably agreed on the pre-eminence of the ethical aim, yet because the predominant emphasis in schooling has always been placed on the achievement of cognitive objectives, the outcome is a system which is decidedly unethical. The sympathy of the over-intellectualizing educationist is with these cognitive objectives. True educators are more generous in their sympathies: 'Education is all one with living', 'By their deeds shall ye know them', 'Aimez l'enfance', 'No impression without expression', 'Hearts, not heads in school' – these are only a few of their typical utterances. While paying lipservice to them in public, the educationist is too often privately convinced that they are really nothing more than sentimental slogans, which is why he is so peculiarly impotent when it comes to finding a formula to fit the demand for 'free secondary education for all'.

If the leaders of the monstrous regiment of educationists have their way, and the indications are that they will, we must expect to be led once again up the same blind alley which has brought us to this present pass. The medieval Schoolman's insistence on the need for logic and grammar as the indispensable tools for systematic inquiry finds its obvious parallel in contemporary curriculum theory. The resurrection of the seven liberal arts under the guise of 'disciplines', 'domains', 'areas of knowledge', 'catagoreal concepts' and 'modes of experience' (believe it or not, you will find them so variously designated in the space of a half a page in *The Logic of Education*) is a typical example of the New Scholasticism. Another is to be found in John Wilson's study *Education in Religion and the Emotions*, a title which promises to throw new light on a neglected field. The search for a rational justification for religious faith provides a perennial theme for philosophers, but the outcome of this one is no Summa, only a bleak taxonomy. As a connected series of arguments his book is calculated to appeal to logicians. The analysis of emotion-words is cleverly done, but somehow the discussion lacks all sense of human feeling (unless it be the relish displayed by the analyst in his own astuteness). As for religion, all that remains is a contentless concept which the average teacher and the layman will find utterly unrecognizable. Indeed, after following its tortuous course to the end it is tempting to conclude that in one sense this is a thoroughly bad book and that the author needs to be reminded that 'Nullum magnum ingenium sine mixtura dementiae fuit':

> Lovers and madmen have such seething brains,
> Such shaping fantasies that apprehend
> More than cool reason ever comprehends.

In another sense, however, both *The Logic of Education* and *Education in Religion and the Emotions* are the kinds of books which educationists and only educationists revel in, the kind which their reviews recommended as 'important'. The trouble is that the rectitude of their discourse is only preserved by keeping itself as aloof from the plight of schoolchildren as that of St Thomas did from the wretchedness of the serfs. It is all so infinitely far removed from the secret ecstasies and terrors, the boredom and excitement, passions and despairs of life as it is lived in the classroom.

'Let us begin by noting that there can be no experience or knowledge without the acquisition of the relevant concepts', say Hirst and Peters. Let us do nothing of the kind.* Instead, let us

---

* 'It may seem strange that the most immediate experiences in our lives should be the least recognized, but there is a reason for this apparent paradox, and the reason is precisely their immediacy. They pass unrecorded because they are known without any symbolic mediation and *therefore without conceptual form*.' Susanne K. Langer, *Mind: An Essay on Human Feeling* (Johns Hopkins Press, 1967) p. 57.

take our cue from their comments on the etymology and changing usage of the word 'education':

> In English the word was originally used just to talk in a very general way about the bringing up of children and animals. In the seventeenth century, for instance, harts were said to delight in woods and places of their first education. . . . With the coming of industrialization, however, and the increasing demand for knowledge and skill consequent on it, 'education' became increasingly associated with 'schooling' and with the sort of training and instruction that went on in special institutions. This large-scale change, culminating in the development of compulsory schooling for all, may well have brought about such a radical conceptual tightening up that we now only tend to use the word in connection with the development of knowledge and understanding[10].

For 'radical conceptual tightening up' read 'constricted outlook' and the point is made. Until our educational thought is deinstitutionalized nothing can prevent our continuing in the role of system-maintenance men. This secular religion needs to undergo a drastic demythologization. If it is utopian to look forward to a time when young harts will once again delight 'as it were in the fair meadow of a congenial and inspiring environment' (as the authors of *The Education of the Adolescent* were pleased to call it as far back as 1926), the least we can do is to register our disapproval of a *status quo* in the schools which, for many, is only too obviously uncongenial and uninspiring.

> Significant change occurs when people stop believing in what may once have been true, but has now become false; when they withdraw support from institutions which may once have served them but no longer do; when they refuse to submit to what may once have been fair terms but which are no longer. Such changes, when they occur, are a product of true education[11].

It is a time to recant.

3 End of an illusion

First, our national life and, more broadly, our culture do in fact predicate certain traits of mind and ways of looking at man and the world. Second, these traits and outlooks embrace both heritage and change, which in turn correspond, though not exactly and certainly in no wooden, perfunctory way, to general and special education, the one concerned with the more slowly changing relationships within knowledge as a whole, the other with its more quickly changing parts. Third, a successful democracy (successful, that is, not merely as a system of government but, as democracy must be, in part as a spiritual ideal) demands that these traits and outlooks be shared so far as possible among all the people, not merely among a privileged few. But, fourth, there exist in fact great differences among people, not only in opportunity, which have been and can be improved, but of gifts and interests, which either cannot be improved so quickly or, in the case of interests, are and should ideally be varied. Our ignorance, which seems to us a widespread ignorance, and our question, which is the question of the nation and age, follow these four steps as a fifth. It is, how can general education be so adapted to different ages and, above all, differing abilities and outlooks, that it can appeal deeply to each, yet remain in goal and essential teaching the same for all? The answer to this question, it seems not too much to say, is the key to anything like complete democracy[12].

Does the problem posed by the Harvard Committee admit of a solution? We can hardly evade it by saying that, as framed by them in 1945, 'the question of the nation and age' is merely a verbal conundrum, an unanswerable riddle. If a solution is to be found, how can the clash between Jeffersonian and Jacksonian principles, between the claims on behalf of 'excellence' and of 'equality', between middle-class and working-class values, between academic and non-academic secondary schooling, ever be reconciled? Are we any nearer to finding more plausible answers to such questions than the high-minded but implausible one propounded in *General Education in a Free Society*?

So far as the American experience is concerned, it appears that the 'wide and deep differences' in national life have, if anything, become wider and deeper during the last quarter of a century, so much so that today, more than ever, 'the supreme need for American education is a unifying purpose and idea'. Yet if no satisfactory answer has been forthcoming it is clearly not for any want of effort in trying to find one. The intervening years have seen a massive expansion of the educational services at all levels, nowhere more spectacularly than in the USA. How massive and how recent may be gauged by the fact that whereas in 1900 only 6 per cent of American boys and girls completed a high school course, roughly half of the entire 17–18 age group (vastly multi-plied since the turn of the century) now goes to college. Despite this, many would say that the expansion in education has not resulted in an improved society; that possibly America is more troubled, divided and sick now than at the start of the century.

In the meantime educational expansion in Britain has been taking place on a rather more modest scale and at less breakneck speed. In general, however, developments have followed the American pattern. Thus, the number of students in higher educa-tion has more than doubled in the past decade (281,000 in 1960, 591,000 in 1970). More pupils have been staying on after the legal school-leaving age, more gaining larger number of O- and A-level passes, more being recruited for teacher training in the colleges of education. From £811 million in 1958–9, public expenditure on the educational services rose to £2,615 million in 1968–9. During the same period, to some extent prompted by the American example, there has been a notable growth of interest in curriculum development (signalized by the setting up of the Schools Council in 1964), in team teaching, in programmed learning and other aspects of an advancing educational technology. It is timely to ask, therefore, whether these varied and costly endeavours will really change the quality of life in our society.

Periods of expansion are characteristically optimistic. With so many plans afoot, the mood tends to be buoyant. In Britain, any suspicions that all is not well with the education system have been allayed by a succession of official reports – Crowther, Newsom, Robbins, Plowden – which between them fostered the impression that major reforms were just round the corner and that every day in every way things were getting better and better. Fads and fashions have come and gone, distracting attention from the crucial issues. Second thoughts on programmed learning, for example, suggest that the early hopes it raised were misplaced; and it may be thought that the same is true of educational television, computer-assisted instruction and other developments which seemed to herald the advent of a teaching revolution. Current moves in the field of curriculum development, likewise, must be viewed as attempts to give a new lease of life to traditional practices rather than to bring about a New Deal by genuine innovation. In Shipman's judgement,

> The separation of the future élite from the majority through the curriculum has seemed a more acceptable way of dividing these two groups than giving them physically separate schooling. The division remains an essential part of the process of social control, ensuring that contrasting expectations are fixed in childhood.
>
> This selection through the curriculum has also appeared in another apparently progressive innovation. The use of radio and television either direct or through magnetic tapes brings the world into the classroom. It bridges the gap between school and the mass media outside. But this development has again been selective. The future élite are still restricted to books while the innovations are introduced for those who will not take external examinations. One group are learning a written culture in school, the other a reinforcement of the audio-visual culture paramount in their lives outside[13].

Again, the recent interest in the applications of organization theory and management studies is largely inspired by the realization that much more sophisticated techniques are going to be needed if the existing system is to be maintained as a going concern, if the expectations of the majority are to continue to be held down to boost those of the chosen few. At present it is not too difficult for those who possess the necessary manipulative skills to fool most of the people most of the time: at a pinch they can always trot out an argument which purports to show that somewhere, somehow, there is a connection between educational expansion, economic growth and social justice.

But their time is running out; the mood is already less genial. As yet, the lurking sense of disenchantment is not widely shared. It is not occasioned solely by the knowledge that, for the first time since the Depression years, many graduates and school-leavers are joining the ranks of the unemployed. It springs rather from the belated recognition that, despite all the progress we have made towards the goal of free secondary schooling for all, the gap between the educationally privileged and the educationally deprived is steadily widening. The faster the advance, the further the prospect of achieving social justice seems to recede. This is part of the penalty we have to pay for pinning too much faith on education as a panacea, and explains why some of our cherished doctrines, 'parity of esteem' for one, 'equality of opportunity' for another, have lost their earlier allure and now look like joining the 'education of the whole man' in the limbo of lost causes.

To be sure, the episcopate of 'the Established Church Scientific' never tires in its efforts to spread the gospel and needs no Inquisition to stamp out incipient disbelief. Education is never short of pushers. Its nostrums, however, no longer carry quite the same conviction they did for previous generations. Whether it be the philosopher's concept of education as 'initiation', the sociologist's of education as 'socialization', or the logician's resurrection of the 'disciplines', it is clear that there is little prospect of bringing about fundamental changes in a system which provides training in leadership for the few and second-best treatment for the many. From Comenius to the present day, the theory and practice of education have been weighted in favour of an intellectually able minority. The illusion of supposing that education might eventually bring about equal treatment for all has only been sustained by the emergence of Christianity's promise of spiritual equality in the sight of God as part of the essential propaganda for spreading the new secular religion. In practice, the humanists' criterion for the estimate of human worth has always been an intellectual one. In adopting this criterion, 'sound learning', as the Scots fondly called it, has invariably favoured the lad o' parts while turning a blind eye on almost everyone else. As religious faith has receded further and further into the background, the greater has been the tendency to push the idea of equality of opportunity into the foreground. 'Free secondary education for all' sounds fine, provided that we do not inquire too closely into the terms on which it is offered. The more closely we inquire, the easier it becomes to see our worship as idolatry. In other words, so long as education is identified with schooling there *can* be no solution to the problem posed by the Harvard Committee.

Not surprisingly, it is from the USA that the demand for

alternative solutions has received its most forthright and articulate expression. Recently there has sprung up a whole literature of dissent: *The Greening of America, The Making of a Counter Culture, Crisis in the Classroom, Deschooling Society, School is Dead, Teaching as a Subversive Activity* – these are some of the more sensational titles. In much the same way that Rousseau's *Émile* may be seen as a necessarily irrational outburst in the Age of Reason, the impact made by this new genre of educational thinking and writing (and already its impact can claim to be considerable) derives its force from a deepfelt disgust for the crass pursuit of affluence, the mindless worship of technology, the Gadarene stampede towards a polluted, congested world, but above all for the futility of the popular superstition which sees education as a commodity obtainable exclusively in schools and colleges. Schools, they argue, have outgrown their purpose. Rich countries have developed an educational establishment which they can hardly afford, and which poorer countries cannot possibly emulate. Schooling reinforces a meritocracy, they think. Worst of all, schooling, as at present practised, takes place in institutions which are as coercive as prisons and mental hospitals.

Needless to say, these authors are a decidedly mixed bunch. Their protest stems from a variety of contexts and causes, and some of them make no secret of being shameless iconoclasts. All share the same penchant for sweeping generalizations, not to mention a blithe disregard for any sort of empirical evidence to support their claims. All of them are guilty of woefully under-estimating the 'dynamic conservatism' of the institutions they seek to overthrow. The alternatives they propose are, for the most part, so unconvincing as to stand little or no chance of gaining popular credibility, let alone acceptance. Of them all, Ivan Illich is in many ways the most enigmatic figure, a curious blend of Roman Catholicism and Marxist zeal who writes in a style that, at best, verges on the hieratic and, at worst, loses itself in turgid rhetoric. Ideas which have remained latent since the days of Kropotkin and William Morris seem to have germinated in this extraordinary mind whose utterances have suddenly become the tabletalk in academic circles throughout the world.

How to account for the commotion which the deschooling movement has undoubtedly caused? One reason might be that the genuine odd-man-out, whether it be Socrates or Marshall

McLuhan, calls attention to himself by his sheer effrontery. He is
the man of genius who propounds a new theory because he refuses
to accept an axiom which no one else has even dared to question.
The fact that these rebels fail to agree among themselves, and that
they often fly in the face of what is generally thought to be common
sense is not to be held against them. By definition, there can be no
'school' of deschoolers.

> In brief [says Ian Lister], deschooling is not a precise concept
> with clear delimitations – nor would its creators wish it to be. It
> is less a concept than a general drift of thinking. Nor could it be
> located within a discipline such as sociology, psychology or philo-
> sophy: indeed, it is one of the greatest strengths of Goodman,
> Illich and Reimer that – unlike many educational thinkers in
> England – they are not the prisoners of any single discipline[14].

What, then, is implied by this 'general drift of thinking'? If for
nothing else, the deschoolers earn credit for bringing into the
open the secret doubts which public faith in education prefers to
conceal and to stifle whenever it can. They bring us face to face
with the Absolute Paradox: either education or schooling – either
the nurture of personal growth or the organized ritual. To para-
phrase Kierkegaard, institutionalized care of the young is incom-
mensurable with the business of learning and growing. Broadly,
the case which the deschoolers are trying to present adds up to
saying that we are all in danger of confusing the shadow with the
substance and hence of supposing that the more schooling we
have the more educated we are certain to be. As Goodman puts it,
'This case is that we have been swept on a floodtide of public
policy and popular sentiment into an expansion of schooling and an
aggrandizement of school people that is grossly wasteful of wealth
and effort and does positive damage to the young'[15]. Wasteful
because learning in abundance is permanently ruled out so long as
it is restricted to what goes on in the classroom; damaging because
the enforced herding together of the young not only isolates them
from the rest of adult society but serves to keep them dependent
on the services provided for them longer than is strictly necessary.
   Whether we call this herding together of the young in special
institutions 'education', 'initiation', 'socialization', 'training', 'discipline', 'conditioning', or even 'indoctrination' is really imma-
terial: in the vast majority of cases we can be sure that its effects

will be permanent and irreversible. Whichever name we care to choose for it, the assumption is that the educative process will deliberately bring about changes in the learner's behaviour; more crudely, that it will be concerned to do things *to* him rather than trust him to do things for himself. Admittedly, this distorts the process somewhat, but in the sense in which it is normally used, the verb 'to educate' is active only, or at any rate mainly, for the teacher, not for those who are *in statu pupillari*. It seems that the deschoolers, like the child-centred theorists before them, are urging the need for greater freedom for the individual to educate himself – a freedom which becomes increasingly important as schoolchildren grow older, no longer helpless and inevitably dependent infants, but teenagers eager to 'do their own thing'.

No less serious is the charge that the education system has become a monopolistic enterprise which controls every aspect of our daily lives. We forget all too easily that many of its features which have come to be taken for granted, compulsory school attendance for instance, were bitterly opposed by eminent Victorians. Says Reimer:

> The school system has thus amazingly become, in less than a century, the major mechanism for distributing values of all kinds among all the peoples of the world, largely replacing the family, the church and the institution of private property in this capacity. In capitalist countries it might be more accurate to say that schools confirm rather than replace the value-distribution of these older institutions. Family, religion and property have such an important influence on access to and success in school that schooling alters only slowly and marginally the value distributions of an earlier day. Jefferson put it well when he said, in arguing for public schools, that by this means we shall each year rake a score of geniuses from the ashes of the masses. The result of such a process, as the English aristocracy learned long before Jefferson, is to keep the élite alive while depriving the masses of their potential leaders[16].

The subtle ways in which our value systems are dominated by the school system can easily be demonstrated. One of the clearest illustrations is to be found in *Education and the Working Class*:

> Education then dictated marriage. Not altogether, and not exclusively, but that is the emphasis one wants to make. When

we asked those who were unmarried what qualities they were looking for in a partner, they tended to begin with an educational 'qualification'. If the woman had her A-level, then she wanted a husband who had his, or more. If she had a degree, then this was her minimum. Perhaps it was good sense, but it seemed rather an odd insistence. There are, need it be said, many other valuable qualities. . . . Some had tried boy or girl friends who had only gone to secondary modern schools, but felt they were too far apart. It was hard to find a point of contact from which to broaden the relationship, and raw attempts to 'educate' were disastrous. 'As a matter of fact the girl I was engaged to hadn't been to a grammar school and she broke it up. The educational differences had a lot to do with it. I tried to get her to broaden her ideas and improve herself, but she wasn't prepared to do that.' The educational lines were too firm for most sexual relationships to break through[17].

Leaders of the deschooling movement are not to be blamed because they offer no specific programme of reforms. In so far as they can be said to have an agreed policy it is one based on the conviction that the surest way of making resources for learning more widely available is by playing down and debunking the importance attached to formal schooling. The badness of institutional fit resulting from the carryover into the late twentieth century of a type of organization and a set of bureaucratic regulations designed to meet the conditions of nineteenth-century mass production clearly needs to be remedied. If there is something rotten in the state of education where else shall we look for the source of the malaise if not in the organization of the school itself? Is the 'hidden curriculum' which Illich and Musgrove alike complain of a reminder of the truth, that the medium is the message? And if so, how is that message to be construed?

In order to see clearly the alternatives we face, we must first distinguish education from schooling, which means separating the humanistic intent of the teacher from the impact of the invariant structure of the school. This hidden structure constitutes a course of instruction that stays forever beyond the control of the teacher or of his school board. It conveys indelibly the message that only through schooling can an individual prepare himself for adulthood in society, that what is not taught in school is of little value, and that what is learned outside of school is not worth knowing. I call it the hidden curriculum, because it constitutes the unalterable framework of the system, within which all changes in the curriculum are made.

The hidden curriculum is always the same regardless of school or place. It requires all children of a certain age to assemble in groups of about thirty, under the authority of a certified teacher, for some 500 to 1,000 or more hours each year. It doesn't matter whether the curriculum is designed to teach the principles of fascism, liberalism, Catholicism, or socialism; or whether the purpose of the school is to produce Soviet or United States citizens, mechanics or doctors. It makes no difference whether the teacher is authoritarian or permissive, whether he imposes his own creed or teaches students to think for themselves. What is important is that students learn that education is valuable when it is acquired in school through a graded process of consumption; that the degree of success the individual will enjoy in society depends on the amount of learning he consumes; and that learning *about* the world is more valuable than learning *from* the world[18].

To the traditional-minded, Illich's reasoning is fated to seem perverse although, as was pointed out earlier, impartial socio-logical analysis is inclined to agree with it. Still, a society which has invested so heavily in its educational services is far too deeply committed to acknowledge that they are founded on nothing better than an illusion. 'What's wrong with compulsory schooling anyway?' it asks defiantly.

References

1. Theodore Roszak, 'Education contra naturam' in R. Gross and P. Osterman (eds.), *High School* (New York, Simon & Schuster, 1971), p. 68.
2. Jean-Jacques Rousseau, *Émile.*
3. Herbert Read, *A Coat of Many Colours* (RKP, 1945), pp. 59–60.
4. Sören Kierkegaard, *Journals.*
5. Ivan Illich, 'The alternative to schooling', *New York Saturday Review* (19 June 1971).
6. Quoted in the *Arts Guardian* (29 September 1971).
7. L. C. Taylor, *Resources for Learning* (Penguin Books, 1971), p. 15.
8. F. Musgrove, *Patterns of Power and Responsibility in English Educa-tion* (Methuen, 1971), pp. 146–7.

9. Everett Reimer, *School is Dead* (Penguin Books, 1971), p. 52.
10. P. H. Hirst and R. S. Peters, *The Logic of Education* (RKP, 1970), p. 23.
11. Everett Reimer, op. cit., p. 96.
12. Harvard Committee, *General Education in a Free Society*, 1968 ed. (Harvard University Press, 1945), p. 93.
13. M. D. Shipman, *Education and Modernization* (Faber, 1971), p. 188.
14. Ian Lister, *The Concept of Deschooling and the Future of Secondary Education* (Amsterdam, European Cultural Foundation, 1971).
15. Paul Goodman, *Compulsory Miseducation* (Penguin Books, 1971), p. 11.
16. Everett Reimer, op. cit., p. 27.
17. Brian Jackson and Dennis Marsden, *Education and the Working Class* (RKP, 1962), p. 169.
18. Ivan Illich, *New York Saturday Review*, loc. cit.

Section II

WHAT'S WRONG WITH SCHOOLING ANYWAY?

The unrealistic sound of these propositions is indicative, not of their utopian character, but of the strength of the forces which prevent their realization. The most effective and enduring form of warfare against liberation is the implanting of material and intellectual needs that perpetuate obsolete forms of the struggle for existence.

Herbert Marcuse, *One-Dimensional Man*

WHAT'S WRONG WITH SCHOOLING ANYWAY?

1 Schooling conditions everyone to the acceptance of schooling as necessary

Of all the points in the argument, this is the one which is most difficult to get across. Far from striking us as odd, the fact that school is the only institution in which everyone is legally compelled to spend ten or more years of his life has come to seem perfectly natural. We forget that compulsion is less than 100 years old and that the leaving age was raised to eleven as recently as 1893. We forget J. S. Mill's warning in his *Essay on Liberty*:

> A state which dwarfs its men in order that they may be more docile instruments in its hands, *even for beneficial purposes*, will find that with small men no great thing can be accomplished. The Mischief begins when, instead of calling forth the activities and powers of individuals and bodies, it makes them work in fetters, and bids them stand aside, and does their work for them.

We forget Mrs Baker. Remember Mrs Baker? Her book *Children in Chancery* caused quite a stir at the time of its publication, being a blow-by-blow account of the series of legal actions, lasting from 1952 to 1962, in which she sought to establish her right to educate her children at home. Even at the time, public opinion seemed to waver between lukewarm sympathy and sheer indifference for a cause which the vast majority of parents had long since given up as hopeless. The cause itself might be just;

but the man or woman who fights for it is only asking for trouble. This is the consensus view. The case of *Baker v. Norfolk Education Committee* is significant because, as E. G. West points out:

> it shows how far we can become slaves of conformity and suppress individuality and spontaneity by our mistake of concentrating power instead of dispersing it. In reading this case one gets the distinct impression that Mrs Baker's main shortcoming in the eyes of the local authorities was not her 'failure' to educate her children according to their needs but her refusal to obey official commands and to show exact equality with other parents[1].

Even the moral courage of a Socrates, it seems, is nullified by the socio-political forces embodied in the education system. Schooling creates its own norms of behaviour and those who refuse to toe the line are classed as deviants and treated accordingly. As a result, it is virtually impossible to find anyone nowadays who has not been subjected to a lengthy process of formal schooling, which means that belief in the necessity and propriety of such processing has become wellnigh universal.

We tend to have faith in the processes we are subjected to – to the extent even, as educationists have made great play of in connection with the practice of streaming, of fulfilling the prophecies made about us by these processes. (It is now generally agreed that once pupils are labelled 'bright' or 'dull' the tendency is for them to behave accordingly.) No one can deny that 'School prepares [children] for their future in a world of organization and bureaucracy. . . . Punctuality, quiet, orderly work in large groups, response to orders, bells and timetables, respect for authority, even tolerance of monotony, boredom, punishment, lack of reward and regular attendance at place of work are habits to be learned in school'[2]. The end products of this process will, not unnaturally, defend it. We are schooled to accept the process of schooling as both inevitable and necessary.

Let us examine some of the conditions which make modern schooling so extraordinary. The first, compulsory attendance to the age of sixteen or beyond, in some ways represents a flat denial of the concept of children's rights. The notion, both popular and legal, that children have rights which need to be respected and protected is of fairly recent origin. According to one view, there was no such thing as 'childhood' until late medieval times: it was only when infant mortality rates declined that parents could afford the luxury of loving their little ones. As for 'adolescence', it is almost certainly an invention of nineteenth-century industrial urbanization. The Factory Acts designed to mitigate the evils brought about by the exploitation of cheap child labour were the precursors of the Education Acts which invoked the principle of compulsory school attendance. Initially, government intervention was intended to be protective: in the long run, its effects have been to delay the assumption of adult roles to the point where protection becomes overprotective. By degrees, the *patria potestas* which enabled the Roman father to treat his sons and daughters as personal possessions, if necessary as chattels, has been transferred in a large measure to the state. On the whole, the imposition of bureaucratic controls has ensured that children are cared for more humanely than used to be the case and that they are not exposed to ill-treatment from brutal parents or unscrupulous employers. In this sense, the gain in children's 'rights' has been enormous: in another, their status has arguably been diminished. There is, for example, no place now for the kind of autonomy enjoyed by schoolboys in less paternalistic days.

> The eighteenth-century public school has been described as an enormous society of boys between the ages of eight and eighteen governed by an unwritten code of its own making, an almost free republic of 100, 200 or 500 members. The traditional view was that outside lessons schoolboys had the right to freedom from adult control. A boy had to attend at meals, prayers, classes and bedtime, otherwise he could go where he liked and do as he pleased.

> As a result of their freedom over many years, Victorian youth in all the public schools inherited a code of rights covering the use of its leisure, whether it was in sport or games, fighting, fishing, hunting, fagging or dramatics. Both juniors and prefects defended these rights against all comers, even the headmaster[3].

It is true that there was never any question of the nineteenth-century elementary schools being allowed to develop as little republics, for they were bound to a code which effectively **ruled** out anything in the way of pupil participation, but the gradual encroachment on the public schoolboy's right to run his own affairs must be seen as part of a general movement in the direction of total regulation of the learner's behaviour. The paternalistic policy, of course, justifies itself as being in the pupil's own interests. It depends on the belief that adults know best what is good for children.

Even in the relaxed atmosphere of the nursery school it has been estimated that under-fives are constrained (i.e. forcibly prevented from doing as they please) ten times per hour. The built-in constraints of the average day school are a good deal more severe, and continue until pupils reach the age when they are capable of having children of their own, of voting, of fighting and dying for their country. From California to Kiev, schoolchildren are required to 'freeze' on the spot once the teacher's whistle blows, then form into straight lines and march into school like so many clockwork mice. Once inside, freedom of speech, freedom of movement, freedom of assembly and freedom of thought (despite disclaimers to the contrary) are denied to them. Any attempt on the pupils' part to organize themselves as a pressure group is ruthlessly stamped out, and anyone who aspires to the role of a juvenile shop steward is immediately singled out as a troublemaker and dealt with accordingly. As the *Little Red School Book* rightly noted, 'In most schools corridors are places for chasing children out of or through. . . . Most playgrounds look like car parks or prison exercise yards. . . . Most classrooms look like waiting rooms.'

The waiting room simile is apt because it underlines another peculiar condition of modern schooling, the segregation of the young from the rest of society. It would be an exaggeration to say that the child is somehow transformed by the separation from his family and the initiation into the impersonal routines of the classroom. Though it is true that the pupil has to spend a large proportion of his waking hours in school, school can hardly be called a 'total' institution.

The school itself, as custodian of even larger numbers of people, for increasing proportions of their life span, for an ever-growing number of hours and interests, is well on the way to joining armies, prisons and insane asylums as one of society's total institutions. Strictly speaking, total institutions are those which totally control the lives of their inmates, and even armies, prisons and asylums do this completely only for certain inmates.

Only vacationless boarding schools could strictly be called total institutions, but perhaps the strict definition gives too much attention to the body and too little to the mind and spirit. Schools pervade the lives and personalities of their students in powerful and insidious ways and have become the dominant institution in the lives of modern men during their most formative years[4].

Statements of this sort are such a blend of overstatement and truth that it is possible to agree whole-heartedly with parts of them and disagree violently with others. To add to the confusion, sociologists and psychologists are by no means unanimous in their views about the nature of so-called 'total' institutions or about their effectiveness in forming people's personalities. In general, there is little doubt that public schools *do* succeed in stamping pupils with a recognizable brand image of 'character' and that orphanage children exhibit personality traits quite different from those reared at home. There is no doubt, either, that the scope* and pervasiveness† of the school's sway over the lives of its pupils have steadily widened. The gradual assumption of responsibilities formerly discharged by parents – school meals, medical care, school uniform and the rest – is but one aspect of this increase in the exercise of normative controls. Another, less obviously notice-able, is the erosion of the learner's responsibility for making his own decisions and his own mistakes. As we have just seen, it used to be understood that the teacher's job was only to teach: today his role could be described as all-purpose.

However, the main reasons for thinking that the segregation of schoolchildren from the rest of society is an artificial contrivance are really quite different. That the hiving-off has inevitably led to the formation of a separatist youth culture and the phenomenon which we have come to know as the generation gap is one reason. Another is that the gradual lengthening of school life has kept older pupils in a state of dependence, this at a time when the trend towards early physical and emotional maturity is more pronounced than it has ever been. Lastly, and most damningly, the conclusion

* '*scope* – the number of activities in which members are jointly involved.'
† '*pervasiveness* – the range of activities both within and outside the school for which it sets standards and has clear expectations' Frank Musgrove op. cit. p. 21.

to which we are driven must be that whatever the ostensible motives for requiring full-time attendance to the age of sixteen, the undeclared purpose is simply to keep young people off the streets because there is nowhere else for them to go. In the many mansions of modern society the school serves as an antechamber. The irony of it is that whereas the society they will enter is permissive, schooling remains authoritarian. For some, the protracted period of waiting is so tiresome that they vote with their feet and become dropouts. For others, the risks involved in trying to escape are too great and the only refuge to be found is in daydreaming. For most, of course, the response is one of cheerful acceptance: going to school, they say, is 'not so bad' after all and there is no point in trying to make it out to be worse than it is. To remain *in statu pupillari* is *not* the same as serving a prison sentence, (even if it does feel like it to some teenagers).

Schooling constrains its subjects physically and mentally; it isolates them from society; and thirdly it continuously monitors their performance. In no other institution is the regulation and control of human behaviour applied so consistently or so rigorously. The state of affairs in the English grammar school described by Lacey, King *et al* [5], in which too many pupils compete for too few rewards, exemplifies in an acute form a general characteristic of schooling. It is a process in which, in the nature of things, there are few winners and many losers. It is not merely the disadvantaged child who finds himself in a learning situation which is essentially punitive. And if this sounds like a sweeping generalization how are we to explain away the preoccupation of educational theorists (and teachers) with problems of discipline and punishment?

This process – with its threefold arms of constraint, isolation and monitoring – produces an end result which can be given in one word – compliance. The ease with which innocent minds can be moulded more or less at will, by suggestion, by intimidation, by hero worship and by a variety of other means, has always been acknowledged. An early and canny argument in favour of taking advantage of it is to be found in the *First Book of Discipline*:

> The children of the poore must be supportit and sustenit on the charge of the Church till tryell be tackin whether the spirit of docilitie be fund in them or not. Yf thei be fund apt to letteris

and learnyng then may thei not (we meane neathir the sonis of the riche nor yit of the poore) be permettit to reject learnyng, but must be chargeit to continew thair studie so that the Commonwealth may have some comfort be them.

The fact that in sixteenth-century Scots parlance 'docility' had much the same meaning as 'educability' now cannot dispel the suspicion that it also implied a willingness to obey orders without question or complaint. In short, there certainly *is* a sense in which it can be said that *l'éducation peut tout* for nothing is more obvious to observers of foreign school systems than their success in conditioning children to perform like automata. By exploiting the 'spirit of docility' it is possible to get children to do almost anything. But for this, compulsory schooling would never have been possible. Since the early days of popular education habits of sitting still, keeping mum, and following instructions have become so deeply engrained that they have become established as norms of correct conduct (and good manners), norms which are only now being challenged by student activists and the dissident advocates of 'pupil power'. The pity of it is that we can see the undesirable side effects of schooling in other countries but not in our own. We are all pressed men who have come to love our quarters below decks.

References

1. E. G. West, *Education and the State*, 2nd ed. (Institute of Economic Affairs, 1970), p. 193.
2. M. D. Shipman, *Education and Modernization* (Faber, 1971), p. 36.
3. F. Musgrove, *Patterns of Power and Responsibility in English Education* (Methuen, 1971), p. 80.
4. Everett Reimer, *School is Dead* (Penguin Books, 1971), pp. 24–5.
5. C. Lacey, *Hightown Grammar* (Manchester University Press, 1970). R. A. King, *Education* (Longmans, 1969).

2 Schooling is an impersonal process

Advocates of deschooling should beware of setting up a straw man. It is mischievous to pretend that schools are worse than they really are. Even if we accept the working definition of schools as 'institutions which require full-time attendance of specific age groups in teacher-supervised classrooms for the study of graded curricula', it will be easy to point to any number of exceptions to the rule: non-graded schools, 'setting', team teaching, extra-curricular activities, group work, individual projects etc. This is another way of saying that many of the reforms advocated by the deschoolers are already being tried out in contemporary practice.

Yet the very fact that the school handles large numbers of children necessitates a certain standardization in its organization and methods. Schooling is essentially a collective experience, a separate culture. The cells of which it is composed – 'classes', 'forms' (the names are significant) – are secondary groups which cannot hope to match the intimacy of personal relationships in a primary group like the family. While it may be pleasant to think of the teacher as being *in loco parentis* the formal requirements of his profession in the service of a bureaucratic system tend to make the thought more of a pleasant dream than a reality. Attention to individual differences is supposedly one of his chief responsibilities; but if the teacher of a class of 40 did nothing else he could not devote more than one minute to each of his pupils in the course of a single period. In the past, not surprisingly, schools have preferred to concentrate on the task of formal instruction with its clearcut aims, methods and measures of achievement. As a result, for the great majority of pupils, school life began as a name on the register and ended as a number in the examination hall.

With educational theory setting its sights higher and higher, the teacher's role has become anything but clearcut. In practice, he may still think of himself first and foremost as an instructor, not a makeshift father figure, guide, philosopher and friend, but whether or not he has any aspirations in this latter direction his professional ethic has become inflated, (though strangely not enhanced) with the passage of time. In addition, to offset the facelessness of life in the classroom, the authorities, as well as voluntary agencies, have felt obliged to organize an intricate array of ancillary services designed to bring about closer liaison between school, home and neighbourhood: education welfare officers, parent-teacher associations, school care committees, social workers, child guidance experts, counsellors, youth employment officers and so on. As a combined operation for the rescue of derelict children all this is praiseworthy; but officialdom, not content with looking after waifs and strays, has spun and spread its web of paternalism ever wider, and the network continues to grow. The *raison d'être* for this growth by division of labour appears to be that it is unrealistic to expect the teacher to discharge his responsibilities *in loco parentis* without the support of several kinds of specialists in child care. If the latter can be co-ordinated as a team, this may lighten the teacher's burden, though judging by the way things are going this is not happening and the outcome seems to be a case of 'too many cooks'. In the jargon of the day the talk is of 'interprofessionalism' and 'role diffuseness' – terms which might well be translated as 'overlapping of function' and 'duplication of effort'. The truth of the matter is that 'Each profession lacks such clearly recognizable and obviously indispensable techniques and insights as are possessed by the pilot or the surgeon; and no one can be certain what knowledge, skills and attitudes are "essential" for the practising teacher or social worker'[1].

Looked at objectively, this hierarchy of welfare-statism centred on the school must be seen as resulting from a policy of educational imperialism which is constantly seeking to extend its do-good influence over the upbringing of the young. Its falsity lies in the assumption that the wholeness of personal relations is equal to the sum of its parts. Between them, the most dedicated of staffs, aided and abetted by the most proficient specialists, cannot convert the school into a home from home. In a truly educative society, as in the Athenian city state, *paideia* (the classical Greek term for the upbringing of children) is possible and natural because there is complete harmony between family, religious, political and economic institutions. By contrast, schooling as we have come to know it involves an artificial hiving-off from the rest of society.

At the heart of the matter is a conflict of desires, on the one hand those of the parents, on the other those of the educational authorities.

The parental role emphasizes acceptance of the child, warts and all, irrespective of standards of performance or of levels of attainment. . . . For the teacher the situation is different. However much her training may have emphasized the need to give individual attention to the whole child, her role imposes upon her a more objective, achievement-oriented approach, where performance will be evaluated and the claims of the family and the child adjudicated. . . . At one level, the family and the school, the latter representative of community values, committed to the principles of social justice, the former properly and selfishly concerned primarily with the welfare of its own members, stand in clear opposition to one another[2].

This opposition, in turn, finds its expression in a teacher–pupil relationship which remains one of dominance–subordination even in schools where so-called progressive methods are the rule. As Willard Waller noted long ago,

> The teacher represents the adult group, ever the enemy of the spontaneous life of groups of children. The teacher represents the formal curriculum, and his interest is in imposing the curriculum in the form of tasks; pupils are much more interested in their own world than in the dessicated bits of adult life which teachers have to offer. The teacher represents the established social order, and his interest is in maintaining that order, whereas pupils have only a negative interest in that superstructure. Teacher and pupil confront each other with attitudes from which the underlying hostility can never be altogether removed. Pupils are the material in which teachers are supposed to produce results. Pupils are human beings striving to realize themselves in their own spontaneous manner, striving to produce their own results in their own way; in so far as the aims of either are realized, it is at the sacrifice of the aims of the other[3].

No one should be deceived by the state of affairs which obtains in schools where the spirit of docility still prevails. There, friendliness and give-and-take between teacher and pupils may be the rule. Much more significant are the near riot conditions existing in 'tough' schools, where the most that can be bargained for is an uneasy truce and where the threat of open aggression is never far away. Why so? Because for all its ugly manifestations, this unruliness is all that remains of an autonomous life-style which was once universal, a vestigial reminder of an uninhibited independent frame of mind which has been progressively eroded since the introduction of compulsory schooling. However far-fetched it seems to argue that schooling is an affront to personal liberty, existentially this is how it *feels* to many pupils – and not only to those whose language answers to Bernstein's 'restricted code'. Falling in with the orderly routine and carefully regulated way of life in the classroom may be easy enough for the majority: for others it goes against the grain. The young ruffian who refuses to come to heel ('Make me!') should be our example. Instead, we make an example of him.

Among other things, this explains why so many young teachers begin their professional careers full of lofty ideals – resolved, for example, never to resort to corporal punishment – only to shed them within a year or two and agree that a policy of 'getting on top of the little horrors' is the only one with any survival value. Moral education, character training and all the other professed aims of educational theory reduce themselves to a sad mockery in everyday practice. Too often, as a teacher, you need to steel your nerves before stepping into a classroom full of D-stream adolescents. Too often, as a pupil, you need to die a little, grin and bear it, biding your time until you are saved by the bell.

References

1. M. Craft, 'A broader role for colleges of education', in J. W. Tibble (ed.), *The Future of Teacher Education* (RKP, 1971), p. 33.
2. W. Taylor, 'Family, school and society' in M. Craft, J. Raynor and L. Cohen (eds.), *Linking Home and School* (Longmans, 1967), p. 236.
3. Willard Waller, *The Sociology of Teaching* (New York, Wiley, 1932). (Cf. E. Hoyle, *The Role of the Teacher* (RKP, 1969), p. 44.)

3 Schooling is lacking in opportunities for worthwhile activity

If 'lessons' are no longer the sole business of the school they occupy the greater part of its time. This is partly because lessons are the activity most suited to the eggbox nature of a school building designed to accommodate large numbers of children in separate classrooms, each graded and containing its manageable quota. For this reason, schooling is still for the most part a sedentary occupation. To be deskbound may be a fitting fate for the middle-aged, but not for teenagers.

One reason for the assertion that schooling is lacking in opportunities for worthwhile activity, then, is that the process reserves its favours and rewards for the future scholar, not the would-be man of action. Its criteria of worth are arbitrarily intellectual. True, physical training, organized games, drama, music, art and craft, technical subjects and the like afford some relief for those who are not academically inclined but in general school attendance means sitting still, 'paying attention' and carrying out someone else's instructions. Extracurricular activities provide outlets for the pent up energies of pupils, though it should be noted that these do not flourish in most non-academic secondary schools. In any case, if extracurricular activities are considered to be so important why should they be treated as extras? The answer is obvious: because the school's working day is so preoccupied with the acquisition of cognitive skills that it has no time, and very little use, for affective or kinaesthetic learning. That is why, when the bell goes and the pressure is turned off, many adolescents look for ways and means of letting off steam – the discotheque, the street gang, the football excursion, whatever turns them on.

This is not to say that the school is always hopelessly out of touch with the secret aspirations of its pupils. It is the urban environment, not the school, which so limits the possibilities for physical adventure; the media of a technological society which numb the desire for intellectual adventure. The housing estate, no less than the classroom, denies access to the kinds of satisfaction they seek. Outside the school, the law is always waiting for them to put a foot wrong; inside they are restricted by a curriculum which strikes them as at best tame, at worst irrelevant. For some, the only way of finding adventure is to join the ranks of the young offenders.

The efforts of headmasters like R. F. Mackenzie to make mountaineering and sailing an integral part of the curriculum, so graphically reported in his book *A Question of Living*, show how difficult it is to provide opportunities for adventure seekers in a state school. At every turn such efforts are blocked by the official objection that mountaineering and sailing cannot count as 'subjects'. This objection, moreover, is now being endorsed by those curriculum theorists who stress the importance of the development of knowledge as being central to education. Thus Hirst and Peters: 'Our sympathies are with the progressives in their emphasis on motivational factors in education, to which they drew attention with their talk about the needs and interests of children. But our conviction is that this kind of motivation, which is crucial in education, is unintelligible without careful attention to its cognitive core'[1].

Intentionally or not, the reference to the progressives' 'talk about the needs and interests of children' is faintly insulting; after all, from Pestalozzi to A. S. Neill, progressive educators have earned credit the hard way for what they did, not what they said. There is, too, an air of deliberate disparagement in the reference to 'this kind of motivation' – what other kinds can they be thinking of, one wonders? Despite their protestations of sympathy, it is clear that the only realms of 'knowledge' and 'understanding' which logical empiricists can conceive of are first, last and always intellectual ones. On their own admission, other realms of experience are (to them) unintelligible.

They have a point, of course. The flight from learning in American high schools, where credit was given for courses whose 'cognitive core' was nil, may be taken as a horrid warning of what happens when playway methods degenerate into a free-for-all. On the other hand, the more relaxed discipline of American schools and the easygoing, fun thing approach to formal studies – 'growth before grades' as it used to be called – may be seen as stemming from a popular belief that learning and living ought to go hand in hand.

One of Susan Isaac's many telling anecdotes concerns a little girl and her mother who were walking beside a river when a kingfisher flew past. The child's exclamation of delight died on her lips almost before the blue flash had sped out of sight: 'But that's Nature Study,' she said, 'we do it at school.' So early does the morning frost do its killing work. In the first analysis, as in the last, education is something each of us needs to get for himself.

Reference

1. P. H. Hirst and R. S. Peters, *The Logic of Education* (RKP, 1970), p. 39.

4 Schooling distorts values

When John Holt says that 'Schools are bad places for kids', he is voicing an opinion which is at least as old as Quintilian. The latter was in grave doubt about the advisability of exposing children to the malpractices of the *ludi magister* and the *grammaticus* – Orbilius plagosus and his kind – and only decided that, on balance, the risks were worth taking because his protégé, the orator-to-be, needed the stimulus of an audience and hence the company of other boys. Should Holt's sentence read, 'Schools are bad places for kids *when the methods used in them are bad*', or is there some peculiarly insidious influence in the schooling process itself as the abolitionists would have us believe? How can 'good' schools be 'bad places'?

In venting their spleen on the schools deschoolers seem to forget that the ills they complain of have their origins in society at large. Like any other organization, schools must operate according to a set of rules and there is really no excuse for pretending that these are any worse than those which the churchgoer, the MP or even the golf club member has to abide by. If there is plenty to complain about as regards the persistence of bureaucratic regulations which have outlived their purpose – the insistence on short haircuts for boys, for instance – it has to be acknowledged that, in general, the regimen of British schools rarely reaches the depths of petty absurdity which is evidently possible in the USA.

It seems that children who don't want free milk have been flouting one of the Kansas State regulations. The regulation says very clearly, as parents have now been reminded, that even children who never touch milk must always get into queue for it, pick it up and put it on their trays. If children do this, says the regulation, they are permitted not to drink it[1].

Much more disquieting is the role imposed on pupils by the bureaucratic nature of the school as a formal organization. Frank Musgrove makes the point that children have a knack of taking their schooling lightly, even flippantly, and sees this as evidence of their easy mastery of their role obligations[2]. But this ability to wear a double face has its darker side. Cheerful acceptance of the kind of discipline which holds good during school hours is often a mask which is doffed the moment the pressure is off.

Anyone who has been in the ranks of any of the services is aware of the front that is presented to officers, and how it is often parodied by the person who has just been using it as soon as the officer's back is turned. The same kind of thing takes place in any highly disciplined organization (except perhaps in a religious order; but who knows?) and as it does not seem to militate against the maintenance of that discipline no one worries about it, though individual officers may try to persuade themselves that *their* relationship with men is different. When our concern is not merely with the maintenance of discipline but the development in young people of mature personality and a good character, it matters a great deal. A boy who presents a frank, compliant and pleasing facade to his superiors can acquire the reputation of being honest and co-operative while carrying on *sub rosa* all manner of enormities[3].

Without going so far as to say that schooling is a charade, there is an element of playacting involved in it and also an element of duplicity. There is a continual discrepancy between reality and the claims of the school. Setting an example – affecting to be ultra-moral – is part of their role expectation which teachers find increasingly difficult to fulfil. As it becomes easier for him to see through school regulations the adolescent pupil's role is correspondingly more difficult too.

Although they are now being relaxed, school regulations still reflect a puritanical morality which emphasizes such virtues as subordination (i.e. obedience to the commands of superiors); dependability (i.e. absolute predictability); industry (i.e. working hard for small returns); conformity (i.e. convergent frames of mind); competition (i.e. getting ahead of the others): above all else, fatalism (i.e. resigned acceptance of lowly status). In the past this code of values had the support of the family, the Church and the world of work. Today it finds itself in open conflict with the values of a permissive society.

Within its walled-off enclave the school creates its own norms of behaviour, its own consensus of opinion. Pupils are classified as good or bad mainly in accordance with their performance in the narrow range of symbolic skills prescribed for them. Invariably, the resulting order of merit has a long 'tail' of near failures or failures. For those who come out top the game is highly absorbing and they need no inducement to take it seriously. For those at the bottom failure may well leave a nasty taste in the mouth. Everett Reimer remarks that any system in which men get just what they deserve is hell, but the charge against schooling is that its values are so arbitrary and artificial that the mass of children stand no chance of getting what they deserve. In life as it is lived scholastic standards may not count for much, but anyone who does not measure up to them in school is quickly reduced to the ranks. The dunce's cap may have gone but there are other ways of shaming slackers and labelling misfits – and the labels stick.

> Schools often rely on scapegoats to reinforce internal order. The persistent mischiefmaker is not only punished but is denounced publicly. Similarly the honest and hardworking are given house marks and stars and publicly praised. These acts are often surrounded by elaborate ritual, emphasizing the gravity of the offence or the merit of the exemplary. . . . Life in school is a succession of rewards and punishments teaching children to adjust to large, impersonal organizations in which specialization, competition and objective evaluation within a disciplined context are normal[4].

Mostly punishments, many would say. To scorn delight and live laborious days on the offchance of gaining a few token rewards may be all very well for those who are in the running; otherwise, as Holt puts it, school is one long lesson in 'how to turn yourself off'. The values schools try to inculcate are those which suit its requirements as an organization. Yet among themselves schoolchildren take a diametrically opposed view of those same values. Thus, hard work means one thing at the official level whereas in the underground of pupil opinion it is referred to contemptuously as 'being a swot'. Honesty itself becomes ambivalent, construed in one context as making a clean breast of it, in another as a refusal to 'grass'. Speaking one's mind is called 'cheek', sticking to one's guns is penalized as obstinate disobedience, and making a stand on any issue that is felt to be important is branded as mischief-making. If it sounds like empty rhetoric to call schooling repressive, its Procrustean aspects are plain to see.

To quote Shipman again:

> It is this restraint within an organization from the age of five for seven hours a day, five days a week, for ten years or over that is the key to the control exercised by the school. Moral education is insignificant beside the accumulation of pressures on children as they work in school. At entry to infant school children are taught to behave in an orderly way among crowds of other children. Tears and tantrums are rapidly inhibited. Bells, notices, rules, instructions, assemblies, routines and rituals direct them. Marks, badges, tests and examinations show them their level of performance compared with others. They learn to sit still, keep quiet, move with discretion, compete and co-operate. Rights are gradually acquired and responsibilities given to those judged competent. Staff do not have to plan these pressures. The most progressive school still incorporates them. They are experienced by most children as a normal feature of a school[5].

'Rights are gradually acquired' – but only after they have been taken away at the outset. It is not only tears and tantrums that are rapidly inhibited but very often the child's self-reliance as well. It is common knowledge that many children enter school eager to learn and confident in their own abilities only to leave it discouraged and apathetic. If the achievement of the nineteenth-century elementary school was to train people to suffer in silence while they carried out soulless, repetitive work on the understanding that this was all they would ever be good for, the achievement of 'secondary education for all' in the twentieth century is scarcely less ignoble. What could be more mind-chilling for a young, idealistic teacher, meeting his class of D-streamers for the first time, than to be greeted with the wry admission, 'We're the scruff, Sir'. Yet it happens.

How many pupils retire into their shells and give up long before they leave school can only be surmised. For them, the only *modus vivendi* is to go through the motions of school attendance while looking for more satisfying realms of experience in the outside world. It is arguable, of course, that just as the self-made man, say an Andrew Carnegie, once reached the top despite his lack of formal education, so many succeed in educating themselves despite an ample provision of schooling. If so, it has to be conceded that schooling cramps their style. What happens to those

who have been knocked about from pillar to post so long that they
have learned not only to dislike the whole business of education
but to cease to believe in themselves is anybody's guess.

In all teaching, as the programmers have learned to their cost,
there is one overriding objective: to leave the learner at least as
well disposed to his field of study at the end of the course as he was
at the beginning. There is a fatal and widespread assumption that
this objective is usually achieved. On the contrary, all the indications are that it is not. On this count, more than any other,
schooling has to plead guilty. There is a clear discrepancy between
its professed aims and its actual accomplishments. It professes to
promote self-discipline but it is too preoccupied with problems
of keeping its inmates in order. It professes to attach importance
to moral education, but is chiefly concerned with institutional
morale. It professes to engage in character training but goes about
its business in a way which leaves no one in any doubt that it is
mainly interested in examination results. It professes to give equal
treatment to all, regardless of ability, but its treatment is invariably
differential and reduces many to the status of nonentities.
Avowedly, it favours co-operation but from start to finish it
encourages cut-throat competition. It holds out promises which
cannot be kept. It professes to teach children to think for themselves, to form independent, critical judgements and to show
initiative but in doing so insists that they are not to be trusted with
the control of their own learning. It extols creativity but does its
best to stifle it.

There is a good deal of plausibility in the assertion, often made
by deschoolers, that if the same methods used in training children
to read were applied to the vastly more difficult feat of learning to
speak one's mother tongue the world would be full of stutterers
and dumb people. As it is, the world is full of people who think
of themselves as mentally dumb because they have never re-
covered from the long-term effects of going to school. A system
which so underestimates the capabilities of the average child as to
permanently incapacitate him, and which fails to foster the attributes of inventiveness, resourcefulness, open-mindedness, self-
sufficiency and lifelong learning, cannot long survive. As a ladder
of opportunity it deserves no better than to be called a 'ritual of
rising deception'. In a word, the hypocrisy of schooling lies in the
pretence of equating itself with the process of education.

References

1. Punch, 29 September 1971.
2. F. Musgrove, *Patterns of Power and Responsibility in English Education* (Methuen, 1971), p. 48.
3. W. D. Wills, *Spare the Child* (Penguin Books, 1971), pp. 15–16.
4. M. Shipman, *Education and Modernization* (Faber, 1971), p. 53.
5. Ibid., p. 192.

5 Schooling makes nonsense of the concept of equality of opportunity

Plato's *Myth of the Metals*, signifying that children were destined from birth to be first-, second- and third-class citizens, has been sanctified in educational theory and practice throughout the ages[1]. Latterly it has come under attack mainly from the sociologists who see it as a false doctrine; and as the importance of the part played by environmental influences in determining human intelligence has been increasingly emphasized a rival myth, more in keeping with a way of life which is pleased to call itself democratic, has been fathered upon us.

Back in 1926, the Hadow Report's vision of a bright future for the secondary modern school was radiant with good intentions, though even at the time the overblown language of *The Education of the Adolescent* must have struck many readers as less than sincere. Today, 'parity of esteem' has to be reckoned a hoax. No matter how adroitly we juggle with its strong or weak definitions, 'equality of opportunity', likewise, is a myth.

Opportunity for what, it may be asked? 'To get on in the world', is the status seeker's answer. 'To get more out of life', says a consumer society which tends to equate the quality of life with improved standards of living. In the popular metaphor, education is *the* ladder of opportunity and everyone should have the same chance of reaching the top. Attractive as it is, the argument for 'equality of opportunity' as a means of achieving social justice is illusory in practical terms.

The economic argument, no less impressive on the face of it, urges the need for policies of investment in human capital. An advanced industrial nation needs a broadbased supply of skilled manpower and cannot afford to leave the reservoir of talents in its population untapped: this, briefly, is the burden of all the official reports from Crowther (1959) and Robbins (1963) to the present day. For the individual, so the argument runs, a lengthy school life is the surest way of reaching the high-salaried class. For the state, the surest way of keeping well up in the international economic growth league is to increase expenditure on the educational services at all levels, and to keep on raising the school-leaving age. As insurance policies, neither one nor the other is as sound as we would like to think.

If it could be shown that the money spent on raising the age of compulsory attendance at school paid dividends either in the form of higher standards of general education or in improved vocational training the argument on economic grounds might be taken as unassailable. Apart from the possibility that more pupils may scrape one or two O-level passes of doubtful value, however, the probability is that most of them will learn precious little in the extra year that they could not have learned without it.

There is, in fact, an economic catch in this concept of 'equality of opportunity' and it is this. Schooling costs more the longer it lasts (roughly three times as much for each sixth former as for a place in an infant class; more than ten times as much for each undergraduate). In other words, there is room at the top but not for all. The education system, like the society it serves, is an organized competition in which the winners take, if not all, the lion's share. In effect, the losers – always in a majority – are subsidizing a fortunate minority. The educational services are financed from rates and taxes levied on the entire population but relatively few receive the full benefit from their contributions. The extent of the subsidy can easily be gauged by comparing the amount of public money spent during the school life of an early leaver and the amount spent on that of a boy who stays on to the postgraduate stage at a university.

The following tables are based on educational expenditure in Scotland and I am particularly grateful to my colleague Dr C. E. Cumming (Director, Scottish Educational Costs Project), for the carefully worked estimates in Table 2. Estimates for England and Wales would probably differ only slightly from those given here.

Using these unit costs as a basis, a straightforward calculation gives a tolerably accurate estimate of public expenditure on the

Table 1

	Primary	Secondary (below age 16)	Secondary (above age 16)	University (average for all Faculties excluding maintenance grants)
Recurrent costs *per capita*	£76	£135	£236	£1045
Amortised capital cost per annum	£25	£50	£50	£300
Total *per capita* costs	£101	£185	£286	£1345

Annual per capita costs for Primary, Secondary and Higher Education

Source: Education statistics for the United Kingdom 1969. HMSO Table 42, tables on pp. vii, viii.

school life of different types of pupil. Pupil A attends primary school for 7 years, secondary school for 3 years, then enters the world of work. This type, it should be remembered, represents the great majority (some 60 per cent of the school population in Scotland, roughly 75 per cent in England). Pupil B represents the type who stays on for a fifth or sixth year in a secondary school, leaving after gaining an O- and/or A-level certificate award. Pupil C represents the day-release type who leaves the secondary school after 3 years and goes on to a pre-apprenticeship course. (The annual *per capita* cost for such courses has been estimated at £250.) Pupil D represents the type who stays on to the sixth year in a secondary school then takes an ordinary degree at the university. Pupil E is similar but it may be remarked that this type represents, among others, the prospective specialist subject teachers

Table 2. Estimated total public expenditure on pupils whose school lives are different in length*

Type of pupil	Primary	Secondary (below age 16)	Secondary (above age 16)	University	Total
A	7 yrs	3 yrs			£1260
B	7 yrs	3 yrs	2–3 yrs		£2010
C	7 yrs	3 yrs	(1 yr Pre-apprenticeship) (3 yrs Day-release)		£1750
D	7 yrs	3 yrs	3 yrs	4 yrs	£5990
E	7 yrs	3 yrs	3 yrs	5 yrs	£8640

* In 1969 prices.

in secondary schools. In each case the total has been rounded to the nearest £10.

It should be a chastening thought that the annual outlay on a single undergraduate is greater than that expended during the entire school life of the average boy and girl. If only monetarily, this is élitism with a vengeance!

But would a voucher system ensure fairer shares for all?* In Mark Blaug's opinion, under such a system:

Education would still be compulsory up to a legal school-leaving age but parents would now be free, as with compulsory third party automobile insurance. And compared with a tax rebate, vouchers would have the advantage of helping those who paid little in direct taxation; they could be scaled inversely to income, so that their value would be less, the greater the incomes of parents[2].

* First mooted by J. S. Mill, proposals for a voucher system of state *finance*, as distinct from state *provision* of the educational services, have recently found support from economists. See, for example, E. G. West, *Education and the State*, 2nd ed. (Institute of Economic Affairs, 1970); also A. J. Peters, *British Further Education* (Penguin Books, 1967). Broadly the argument favours free enterprise, with vouchers of equal value for all, which parents and students could 'spend' as and when they wished. An experimental voucher scheme is currently being operated and evaluated at Harvard University.

The voucher proposal, thinks Blaug, is 'pure Mill'. If adopted, would it lead to a proliferation of private schools and a kind of educational Apartheid? Are parents competent to choose? How do we know that the disabilities of the working-class would be mitigated? He concludes that, 'Much more discussion of these questions is needed before we try out the voucher scheme even on a trial basis in a limited area'[3]. All the same, it is difficult to resist the impression that the distribution of resources would be more socially just, and that any attempt to back this impression with empirical proof is cold-shouldered only because an alliance of powerful vested interests and administrative convenience supports the existing system.

It is perfectly true that, from one point of view, the scholar who receives eight times as big a share as the non-achieving early leaver is entitled to preferential treatment because he has proved himself to be capable of benefiting from the advanced courses offered. It is also arguable that even the pittance expended on the reluctant D-streamer is to all intents and purposes wasted upon him. What is not in doubt is the gross discrepancy between the dullard's share and the high-flyer's. This might not be so bad were it not for the fact, which is well documented, that the effects of schooling accentuate any initial differences in ability and aptitude (which appear to be firmly rooted in social class), with the result that the slow learner gets duller and duller while the child who is deemed bright gets brighter and brighter.

From start to finish, schooling is essentially élitist, grading and classifying pupils, favouring those who do well in its eyes, demoting those who do not. Though everyone is on the ladder (always supposing that it is one and the same ladder), it is obvious that its higher rungs are only attainable by climbing over the backs of those who are at the bottom of the pile. And the irony of it all is that we call it a meritocracy! The dropout knows better: he can see, more clearly than most, that the cards are stacked against him and that there are other and more meaningful ways of laying hold on life. If this is the way the game has to be played he wants no part of it.

But for nearly everyone else Plato's 'useful lie' operates only too efficiently. The demand for education has become as compulsive as it is universal. The appetite may be healthy but the food provided – schooling – is ersatz; and the shareout is certainly fraudulent.

Schools have succeeded in ritualizing education because they serve societies which dedicate themselves to consumption, which assume that man wants principally to consume and that in order to consume endlessly he must bind himself to the wheel of endless production. The whole theory of schooling is based on the assumption that production methods will result in learning. They do result in learning how to produce and consume – so long as nothing fundamental changes. As a means of learning to adapt to changing circumstances, production methods are ridiculous. The need to distinguish these two kinds of learning is kept from our attention mainly by our participation in the scholastic ritual[4].

But, then, that is the way the world goes, it will be said. Call it a rat-race, keeping up with the Joneses, or what you will, the education system simply reflects the conditions of life in a highly competitive, materialistic society. Meritocratic schooling may have its faults but when all is said and done is it not preferable to the law of the jungle?

Yet the fact remains that the school, as a selective agency, makes nonsense of the concept of equality of opportunity. Our inability to envisage a more equitable system is the measure of our supine acceptance of the *status quo*. Friedman (1962) Wiseman and Peacock (1964), E. G. West (1965)[5] and other economists have advocated the adoption of universal voucher schemes which would allow of parental free choice in their usage. It is true that these schemes are exceedingly complicated, and that in order to implement them it would be necessary to scrap most of the existing administrative machinery. Here, as everywhere, the forces of system maintenance are dug in so firmly that any plan which looks like involving fundamental changes is immediately pigeon-holed. Yet in practice, a universal voucher scheme would have three inestimable advantages. First, it would be less wasteful of resources than the present monopolistic system (which purports to provide the kinds of learning which are better acquired in the home, in church, on the job, through the mass media). Second, it would guarantee fair shares for all. Third and most important, it would place the responsibility for using educational services where it belongs, on the users.

The fear is, of course, that if legal compulsion were removed the children of irresponsible parents would be the first to suffer. This fear could easily be taken care of by inserting safeguards in a voucher scheme. As West says:

> Much as J. S. Mill wanted the protection of children, even he did not in the end prescribe compulsory state schooling, nor even compulsory private schooling, but only compulsory *education*. Accordingly he held that the state should be interested not merely in the number of years of schooling but in checking the results of education whatever their sources, and he contended that an examination system was all that was necessary. If a young person failed to achieve a certain standard then extra education would be prescribed at the parents' expense. Another sanction which Mill also entertained was to make the right to vote conditional on some minimum degree of education. Under Mill's scheme, if it were operating today, it is conceivable that some children would attempt to attain the necessary standards by much more dependence on television, parental instruction, correspondence courses, evening classes, local libraries etc.[6].

It is a sad commentary on our underdeveloped state of mind that the ideas now being resurrected by deschoolers were neither novel nor controversial to some of the eminent Victorians. Mill at least never made the mistake of putting all his educational eggs in one basket: 'Instruction is only one of the desiderata of mental improvement; another, almost as indispensable, is a vigorous exercise of the active energies; labour, contrivance, judgement, self-control: and the natural stimulus to these is the difficulties of life', he affirmed. If, as the twentieth century draws to its close, it begins to look as if the dream of 'an Utopia inhabited by a self-educated and well-educated labouring population' is further from being realized than it was in the days of the Victorians, compulsory schooling is perhaps largely to blame.

References

1. Plato, *The Republic*, III, 414.
2 M. Blaug, *An Introduction to the Economics of Education* (Allen Lane, The Penguin Press, 1970), p. 307.
3. Ibid., p. 316.
4. Everett Reimer, *School is Dead* (Penguin Books, 1971), p. 53.

5. M. Friedman, *Capitalism and Freedom* (Chicago University Press, 1962). J. Wiseman and A. T. Peacock, *Education for Democrats* (Institute of Economic Affairs, 1964). E. G. West, Education and the State, 2nd ed. (Institute of Economic Affairs, 1970).
6. E. G. West, ibid., pp. 12–13.

6 Schooling discourages independent learning

The ultimate purpose of all teaching is to reach the point where it becomes unnecessary. By contrast, schooling tends to be self-perpetuating. The concept of education as a continuous process – the ideal of lifelong learning as it is coming to be called – is only praiseworthy if somewhere along the line the learner waves goodbye to his instructors and supervisors and takes off on his own.

Schooling never lets go. As we have argued, it continuously seeks to extend its controlling and protective influence, to prolong the learner's state of dependence, to delay the assumption of adult roles – this at the very time when the trend towards earlier maturity is more pronounced than it has ever been. As a result, the credibility gap between educational theory and everyday practice is widening all the time. So persistent is the belief in the need for supervision and control that even the Ph.D. candidate can no longer claim to be his own master. Similarly, most of the earnest talk about the need for promoting self-discipline is largely negated by school regulations which lay down guidelines, prescribe courses of action and generally keep pupils tied to their leading strings.

How to phase out the present teacher-based system and replace it by one which shifts the onus for learning on to the learner himself? In a wideranging review of the possibilities, L. C. Taylor sees the provision of an assorted array of packaged learning materials as the likeliest solution to the problem. As he shows, previous attempts to convert schools into places where self-instruction is not only possible but the rule have petered out, mainly, he thinks, because of inadequate resources. A rapidly advancing educational technology promises to change this situation. Accordingly, 'we should test independent learning thoroughly as an alternative method to teacher-based learning in our secondary schools'[1].

(Significantly, the final chapter of *Resources for Learning* is entitled, 'What hopes?' and the author's last words on the subject are somewhat less than optimistic. 'Shall we find this time that we can fly?' he asks plaintively.)

Leaving aside for the moment the philosophical objections to the notion of learning as a marketable commodity* – objections which apply equally well to books – there are at least four practical difficulties which have yet to be overcome in implementing a package deal policy.

First, the trouble with packages is that they take a great deal of time, expertise and money to prepare and sooner or later need commercial backing if they are to go into large-scale production. Because of this, the supply, and hence the choice, of high-quality, field-tested learning materials is decidedly limited. There is no lack of homemade packages designed to meet the particular needs of teachers in local schools, though most of these might be described as amateurish, cottage-industry productions. Again, there is no lack of commercially manufactured hardware and software: indeed, so proliferate (profligate?) is the welter of supplementary aids on offer that even when they are suitable *and* available for classroom use the average teacher is apt to find them more of a nuisance than a help. Expensive equipment lying idle most of the time is only one example of a chronic inability to make the most efficient use of the technical resources *which are already available*. So long as professional competence remains at its present level no 'package' can expect to justify itself in terms of cost effectiveness. The snag is that full professional competence cannot be achieved until there is a much wider selection of materials which satisfy the three conditions of being educationally suitable, readily available and easy to handle. As things are, we are nowhere near the rates of output which enable Radio 1 (if an example drawn from the world of entertainment is permissible) to run a virtually

---

* 'The transformation of knowledge into a commodity is reflected in a corresponding transformation of language. Words that formerly functioned as verbs become nouns that designate possessions. Until recently dwelling and learning and even healing designated activities. They are now usually conceived as commodities or services to be delivered. . . . Men are no longer regarded as fit to house or heal themselves.' Ivan Illich, 'The alternative to schooling', *New York Saturday Review* (19 June 1971).

nonstop programme of records, cassettes and taped music with a handful of disc jockeys.

A second difficulty arises from the opposition of teachers who tend to regard packages as an infringement of their professional autonomy. In so far as the objection is to packages which are designed to be 'teacher-proof' the opposition is understandable and probably sound. Sound because it raises the question of *quis custodiet* and reminds us of the everpresent danger of entrepreneurial takeovers in the education industry. This is a danger which deschoolers too often make light of or overlook altogether, yet we know that free enterprise is only too eager to cash in on the 'resources for learning' market.

A third and much greater difficulty is that of persuading pupils that it is better for them to work on their own. Having sat at the feet of Sir Oracle for so long, it is not surprising that most of them prefer to be told what to do and how to do it, and feel utterly lost if the teacher suddenly withholds the kind of instructions they have come to expect from him. Teaching as a subversive activity on the lines recommended by Postman and Weingartner, that is to say getting pupils to pose questions without pretending to be able to answer them, or discussing open-ended problems of vital concern for which there are no readymade right/wrong solutions, most emphatically does *not* go down well in the normal secondary school. The academic streams are not alone in wanting to get their money's worth in the shape of good, old-fashioned Herbartian lessons which will help them to pass examinations. Non-certificate pupils, like cripples who have lost the use of their limbs, respond only haltingly and soon fall by the wayside when discussion methods are introduced. The disability is carried over to the undergraduate and even the postgraduate stages where many students, often the very ones who are outspoken supporters of 'participation', make it quite clear that they prefer the well-prepared, well-delivered lecture to seminars and tutorials. The latter have their place, they agree, but for these incorrigible note-takers there is nothing to beat lectures, especially when these are accompanied by a liberal supply of handouts summarizing the main points and listing the essential reading.

Ah well, say the traditionalists, it all goes to show that immature minds are incapable of shouldering the responsibilities for learning what they need to know. Nothing of the kind: the general disability is symptomatic of the debilitating effects of the schooling process itself. The fact that the vast majority are 'hooked' on learning in this way proves nothing. Asked whether they approve of corporal punishment, most schoolchildren will say that they do (at any rate in Scotland where some pupils actually glory in boasting about the number of times they have been given the belt), yet we know that this is merely sad evidence of their being inured to a form of imposed discipline which is morally objectionable and operationally ineffective. It is the same with schooling. In the words of a headmaster who has done more than most to transform his school into a resources-for-learning centre,

> Our exhortation to the class not to wait outside but to 'go inside, sit down and get on with your work' is often a false one. It is hardly surprising that it doesn't work in a system where really the pupils don't know what they are going to do next until the teacher comes in at the door and says, 'Now today we're going to. . . .' A move from the teacher being responsible for completing the work with the aid of the pupil to the pupil being responsible for completing the work with the aid of the teacher could make our pupils feel far more motivated and involved[2].

The greatest of all obstacles in the way of independent learning, however, is to be found in the nature of the school organization. Whereas the university is to a large extent bookbased, with lectures occupying a relatively small fraction of the student's time, school of necessity remains talkbased. Fashionable as it is nowadays to utter encouraging noises about the teacher as a 'manager of learning situations', the physical layout of the classroom, and of the eggbox building as a whole, makes it difficult for him to diverge very far from the tramlines of conventional method. Once the classroom door is closed behind him he may like to think of himself as a free agent, but at the same time he knows that the show must go on, and the 'show', inevitably, tends to be a one-man-band performance addressed to a captive audience. England expects that this day and every day from Monday to Friday during termtime every teacher will do his duty; and the surest way of letting everyone see that he is doing it is to keep on talking most of the time. The pupils expect it; their parents expect it; and so, for the most part, do his superiors and employers.

It is true that talking too much is a weakness commonest in

nervous young teachers and that it is often outgrown by the more
experienced ones; true, also, that modern methods of training do
everything possible to eradicate it before students qualify for their
first appointments. Despite all this, it persists.

So far we have discussed four main obstacles to independent
learning: the fact that suitable packages are in short supply, the
opposition of teachers, the disability of pupils (and students), and
the restrictive influence of the school as an organization. The ways
in which these combine to frustrate innovation in the curriculum
can be illustrated by recent developments in the field of programmed learning.

Let us look at what happens to programmed learning in schools
when a teacher who is both knowledgeable and well disposed
decides to use it. Given such a paragon, given also a veritable
laboratory of sophisticated equipment, plus a plentiful store of
programmes, tapes, cassettes, concept films, etc., what happens?

The first thing that happens is that this paragon of ours finds
himself cast in the part of an odd man out. His *modus operandi*
simply does not fit in with the smooth running of the school nor
with the cut-and-dried methods employed by the rest of the
staff.

> Because we have to group boys in classes of roughly equal size
> and assign masters to them, we are forced at present into con-
> structing a timetable in which everyone changes classes at
> defined moments. The bell is king. It demands that we learn in
> episodes of rigid, equal length. It cuts across our brightest and
> our dimmest moments indifferently. The timetable becomes a
> sort of solemn Mad Hatter's tea party. No matter what, how or
> where, when the bell goes we must all move round and face, in
> any old order, one dish or another, on the table before us. It
> may be necessary; it is certainly bizarre[3].

For the sake of argument, let us suppose that this schoolmaster
– or manager of learning situations – decides to soldier on, bell or
no bell. After all, has he not always stressed that one of the advantages of programmes is that pupils can leave off at a given point
and resume working where they left off as and when they please,
and without loss? No matter if the slow learner has only reached
Frame 26 by the end of the period whereas the bright ones have
romped through the entire programme before it was halfway

through, he has plenty more to keep *them* busy. He knows that it is an illusion to imagine that children, even in a so-called homogeneous ability group, can be nursed along at anything like the same pace. But the system under which he is operating makes no allowance for this – these self-pacing pupils of his will receive short shrift when they come to sit an external examination, and those who never get that far are liable to find themselves in trouble in jobs monitored by time-and-motion experts.

Worse still, the system demands that he handles his thirty-odd charges as a *class* and, lo and behold, his class is visibly disintegrating day by day. Only one pupil, at a pinch two, can operate the autotutor at the same time. Catering for individual differences means assigning different sets of programmes and each must have its post-test checked in turn. Before long, queue density becomes more and more of a problem with frequent bottlenecks as pupils wait to have their work examined and to receive fresh assignments. Trying to do justice to all comers makes heavy demands on his ingenuity and patience: he must know exactly what each of them needs, where to find it and when to provide it. This job of singlehanded management is highly complicated: it requires him to act as store keeper, librarian, technician, foreman, consultant, assessor and works manager, all rolled into one. Periodically, it is necessary to call his flock together to explain a key concept or a rule or to view a film of common interest or to listen to a sound tape – with so much going on there is never enough time for everything and practically none for 'straight' teaching.

An outsider looking in on this organized chaos may decide that it is the secondary school's equivalent of the 'integrated day' in primary schools. But as like as not, the Head takes a dim view of it all, and most of his colleagues will probably share the same low opinion. This, they keep telling themselves, is not the proper way for a schoolmaster to go about his business. Too messy by half. In the end the odd man out may conceivably win them over, but it is easy to see that the organizational requirements of the secondary school make this extremely unlikely. More often than not, our paragon will end by being forced to opt out, as like as not to seek pastures new as a college lecturer or a research assistant in a university department which specializes in educational technology.

It is easy enough to complain that this portrayal of the situation

c

is unnecessarily gloomy and that the difficulties in the way of independent learning are slowly but surely being removed as team teaching gets under way and group methods are more widely adopted. Here and there, admittedly, it is possible to point to promising growth points. They are, nevertheless, thin on the ground. It is not only the bell that is king. Secondary schools are geared to a higher authority – university entrance requirements for the front runners, O-level GCE or CSE examinations for the also-rans. So long as these remain the objectives anyone who advocates a changeover to independent learning (with or without packages) can hardly do so without appearing to prejudice the chances in life of the pupils concerned.

It cannot go unremarked that American teachers charter jumbo jets and come in their hundreds to join conducted tours of the primary schools of Oxfordshire, Leicestershire and the West Riding but that few foreign visitors think it worthwhile to go out of their way to see what is going on inside our secondary schools. What makes these primary schools a cause of admiration and envy; and why does the grass look greener on this side of the Atlantic only in this sector? The short answer is that these are the schools and this the sector in which self-activity has been allowed to develop. Instead of bellyaching about the vices of progressive education, reactionary critics should perceive its manifest virtues. To agree that young children learn best and learn most where their self-activity is engaged, and to deny that adolescents can safely be trusted to do likewise is inconsistent to say the least. Logically as well as psychologically, the obvious follow-up to a curriculum conceived in terms of activity and experience is at the secondary stage.

Instead, we allow the restrictive practices inherited from an outmoded and discredited selective school organization and the incubus of an external examination system to dictate terms which effectively nip any prospects of independent learning in the bud. Any spirit of inquiry is stultified. No wonder if the frisky, talkative 7-year-old lambs so often turn into moody, moony sheep by the time they reach the age of fifteen or sixteen. No wonder, either, that the freedoms enjoyed in the primary schools of certain local education authorities have earned for them an international reputation while the image presented by our secondary schools both at home and abroad remains lacklustre by comparison.

References

1. L. C. Taylor, *Resources for Learning* (Penguin Books, 1970), p. 234.
2. *The Resources Centre, Codsall Comprehensive School* 1971–2 (mimeograph).
3. L. C. Taylor, op. cit., p. 27.

7 Schooling provides an inferior learning environment

In the 'Knowledge Society' the school begins to take on the appearance of a culturally impoverished and anachronistic institution.

> One reason why schools are impotent is that they are a bore. (Few curricula can compete with a kestrel.) This is no more than one would expect of schools which . . . are performing their classical task in a radically transformed social environment: no longer information-poor but information-rich, no longer action-rich but action-poor. The Schools Council inquiry into attitudes to school among a national sample of school leavers showed that a majority were oppressed by the monotony of the school: 55 per cent of the 15-year-old boys and 58 per cent of the girls agreed that 'School is the same day after day, week after week'[1].

As an agency for the education and socialization of the masses, the school occupied a position of strength throughout the nineteenth century, and may be thought to have done so until quite recently. So long as the organizational goals of the elementary school were defined as gentling the masses and achieving universal literacy even the lowliest teacher's status as a 'man of learning' was assured, and with no one else to fill it his role as instructor was held to be indispensable. Apart from the church (which hastened to get into the act by establishing its own Sunday Schools), the school was virtually the only accredited institution in the information business. In an age in which learning was practically confined to booklearning, the schoolmaster's monopoly was absolute, a monopoly which was confirmed rather than reduced by the arrival on the scene of public libraries, pulp literature and daily newspapers.

Today, the teacher's status – many would say his credibility – can no longer be taken for granted: in predominantly middle-class areas many parents are as well qualified academically and professionally as he is. As a place where formal instruction is given, the school now faces massive competition from the lateral transmission of information via the mass media and other agencies. It is not simply that the scope of the information business has been vastly enlarged: the nature of 'information' itself, and with it the learning process, have been radically altered under the impact of electronic communication. The failure, inability or unwillingness of the education system to adapt quickly enough to the accelerating pace of social change is discussed at length in the author's book *The School Curriculum* and is, of course, one of the central themes of thinkers like McLuhan who foresee a state of affairs in which everyone, or nearly everyone, will be engaged in the information business.

Granted, the teacher and the school never thought of themselves as the only pebbles on the beach. What they *did* like to think was that they were *primus inter pares*. Now it seems that this modicum of self-importance is to be denied them. Even the university, once the sole, undisputed institution of higher learning, finds its supremacy and its pride of place threatened as, one by one, rival institutions jostle alongside it for a place in the sun. As Musgrove says, 'The problem of schools and universities is to achieve autonomy without losing their bargaining power'[2].

But so far as schools are concerned any bargaining power has already been lost; and far from being only temporary, the loss is almost certainly irretrievable. One reason for thinking that the provision of packaged learning materials is no solution to the problem is that teachers cannot match the sheer professionalism of the media men. Gallant as it is, the attempt to transform the school into a resources centre seems doomed to prove abortive. This is not to say that the attempt is not worth making, simply that in the first instance the main beneficiaries are likely to be the teachers rather than the pupils. The dedicated efforts of isolated schools, of which Codsall Comprehensive is a shining example, prove that a great deal can be accomplished with limited resources and in a building which is not purpose-built. No one will disagree with the headmaster's view that:

> No teacher can function adequately at the high professional level required of him if he makes his own materials unless the school provides a strong supporting service in the shape of equipment, ancillaries and advice, and unless the school finds successful ways of organizing and storing teaching materials and aids, and of discovering and retrieving anything already stored that may be of value to someone else. Once this has been done, any staffroom of teachers could become a fine professional team supporting each other in a variety of ways. . . .
>
> We must be conscious of the implications of the present Schools Council projects, all pioneering new approaches. The directors of these projects have been concerned that teachers should be able to modify or supplement their materials – not in itself easy. None of them is producing a full range of materials, and they are all projects with limited lifespans, one or two of them having come to an end already. The significant question therefore is, once the projects have pioneered approaches and come to an end, who takes over where they left off; and the only answer can be the teachers in the schools themselves. Little consideration has been given to who will train and support them in that[3].

Mr Mitson's point is that in-service training, if it is to be fully effective, should become a continuous process, a regular feature of the teacher's everyday practice, not simply a matter of occasional short intensive courses organized outside the school. Some idea of how this is being done at Codsall may be gathered from Appendix 1 which gives an inventory of the equipment used and flow charts of the activities of the resources centre.

Without in any way seeking to disparage them, however, the best efforts of the finest professional team of teachers are bound to come off second best when set against the slick expertise of the record manufacturers, the film makers and the TV producers. To eyes and ears accustomed to the high standards of presentation of the wide and the small screen, the one-man-band performer cuts a poor figure on the classroom floor (always remembering that most teachers cannot count on the supportive service which a built-in resources centre seeks to provide). To young readers reared on a diet of flashy advertising and glossy magazines the photocopied illustrations and the mimeographed text of 'homemade' workbooks are somehow lacking in allure. Eventually, no doubt, the possibilities opened up by data storage, date retrieval, computerized systems, lasers and other inventions will create opportunities as yet undreamed of in the practical politics of education, but it is difficult to envisage a situation where they will be housed in a building in any way resembling a school.

One of the penalties of living in an age of high technology is that the exercise of power tends increasingly to be centralized, controllable only by large-scale organizations and by specialists. This is true of all forms of communication and applies equally to the jet aircraft, the computer, the radio transmitter or the printing press. Even the costly and elaborate television services run by a local education authority or a university cannot command the resources of money, manpower, skill and equipment at the disposal of the BBC or ITV and must accordingly lower their sights and adjust themselves to less ambitious enterprises. The big guns carry far too heavy a firepower for any individual or group of individuals; and this is why, however regretfully, one is driven to the conclusion that cottage-industry methods cannot cope with the mass-production of learning materials necessary for a viable package solution. Those who find the very idea of packages peculiarly distasteful and who see the traffic and trading in learning materials as typifying a consumer society's crass approach to education may not think this so tragic. Yet without such materials we know that the stock-in-trade of the schools will continue to be chalk and talk, supplemented by books, with the occasional use of audio-visual aids affording, at best, light relief from the drabness of a centuries-old routine.

So long as the school had things all its own way it could close its doors on the outside world. What went on inside its walls was, quite literally, nobody's business but its own. Parents' rights, neighbourhood concerns, employers' interests, public opinion, all were kept firmly at arm's distance if they were not excluded altogether. More so than any other institution, the school tried to keep itself immune to external influences and disturbances and resented any move suggestive of participatory democracy. Its withdrawn position has been commented on by sociologists in other countries, not least in the USA where from the early pioneering days until quite recent times the relationship between the people and their elected school board representatives has always been much more intimate than it ever was, or is, in Britain. The school here remains a partially closed system, devised to meet nineteenth-century conditions, but now shows signs of running down for want of adequate feedback. This is recognized, of course, in the architectural layout of the 'open' school, of which more anon.* The question is whether this outward-looking tendency goes far enough, and whether the next move will be in the direction of an institution answering in one way or other to the description of a 'free' school.

To be sure, the Newsom boy's comment, 'It could be made of marble, Sir, but it would still be a bloody school', has been over-used in discussions on education. At one level of discourse, normally the only one which educationists are prepared to regard as legitimate, this *cri de coeur* seems merely amusing ('Cheeky young devil!'). At another, it may be taken as expressing a genuinely profound insight. It displays a realism quite alien to the philosophy of schooling. The boy is typical not so much of those the education system has rejected as of those who feel in their bones that they have more to gain and nothing to lose by rejecting that system. Their rejection is not rational, at least not in the sense understood by logicians as 'rational': it springs from an intuitive recognition of the subliminal effects of the hidden curriculum. Although they have never heard of him and would not understand a word of what he was saying if they tried to read his works, these schoolchildren are unconscious disciples of Marcuse and have tumbled to a simple truth which looks a good deal less than simple as stated in *One-Dimensional Man*:

> The technical achievement of advanced industrial society, and the effective manipulation of mental and material productivity have brought about a shift in the *locus of mystification*. If it is meaningful to say that the ideology comes to be embodied in the process of production itself, it may also be meaningful to suggest that, in this society, the rational rather than the irrational becomes the most effective vehicle of mystification. . . . Today, the mystifying elements are mastered and employed in productive publicity, propaganda and politics. Magic, witchcraft, and

* See below under 'The open school'.

ecstatic surrender are practised in the daily routine of the home, the shop, and the office, and the rational accomplishments conceal the irrationality of the whole. For example, the scientific approach to the vexing problem of mutual annihilation – the mathematics and calculations of kill and over-kill, the measurement of spreading or not-quite-so-spreading fallout, the experiments of endurance in abnormal situations – is mystifying to the extent to which it promotes (and even demands) behaviour which accepts the insanity. It thus counteracts a truly rational behaviour—namely, the refusal to go along, and the effort to do away with the conditions which produce the insanity[4].

It is the refusal to go along with a system which equates learning with schoolbound learning (i.e. the kind approved of as having a cognitive core) that characterizes the dropout and the early leaver and gives them significance. They are not to be browbeaten or cajoled into accepting the popular mystique. As they see it, schooling provides for the acquisition of skills, knowledge and capacities which they either cannot or do not care to master; while on the socialization side it involves subjection to a kind of treatment which they find demeaning and which defeats its own purpose by keeping them *out* of society. If learning defines itself as that which is prescribed for them in the classroom it is something they feel they can do without.

Are they right? Before venturing any sort of answer it is necessary to decide who *they* are. Broadly speaking, they are the underachievers and the non-achievers. Their failure to do well at school cannot be ascribed to any single cause but in general they answer to Tapper's description:

> The boy comes from a family in which the tradition is to earn one's livelihood through unskilled manual work. This is equally true of his father, mother, brothers, and sisters. He did not even bother to sit the 11-plus examination as it was realized that he had no chance of passing it. He readily accepts his low placement in the secondary modern school. All his friends live in the same district as himself and they form a well-known, troublesome clique within the school. Although he is occasionally in trouble with the teachers he is more inclined to accept the school as a tedious necessity. He is eagerly awaiting his fifteenth birthday when he will be eligible to enter what he considers to be the

real world – the world of work. Everything about the school confirms his own assessment of his probable future role: the condescending or hostile treatment he often receives from the teachers, and the low esteem in which his form, 4D, is held by the rest of the school's pupils[5].

The official view, of course, is that these backward pupils, dissidents, duffers, dunces, passive resisters, or whatever one chooses to call them, represent only an insignificant minority and that they receive more attention than they deserve. This is hardly borne out by statistics showing the close connection between

Table 3*. Class and Streaming

	Middle class	Working class	Total
	per cent	per cent	numbers
LEA grammar schools			
1st stream	75	25	75
2nd stream	65	35	23
3rd stream	75	25	64
secondary modern schools			
1st stream	31	69	246
2nd stream	13	87	116
3rd stream	13	87	175
southern comprehensive			
1st stream	68	32	54
2nd stream	48	52	188
3rd stream	23	77	64
northern comprehensive			
1st stream	27	73	19
2nd stream	9	91	52
3rd stream	16	84	19
Home County bilateral			
1st stream	73	27	47
2nd stream	60	40	20
3rd stream	18	82	39

* Reproduced with permission from Ted Tapper, *Young People and Society* (Faber, 1971).

social class and streaming. As Tapper observes, 'It is not simply a question of the allocation of working-class children to the less prestigeous [sic] schools, for they tend on the whole to gravitate towards the bottom of the pecking order regardless of school type.'

Although there is no way of proving it, the presumption can only be that the 50 per cent plus of malcontents in the Schools Council survey referred to earlier are predominantly working class in origin and background. Unless we are prepared to fall back on a discredited theory of inferior genetic endowment we are driven to the conclusion that the learning environment provided by the schools in some way or other fails to do justice to the abilities and aspirations of a sizeable majority of pupils. To gloss over the problem because the majority remains silent most of the time is worse than ostrichist. It is the non-achievers' dogged 'refusal to go along' which offers the clue that needs to be followed.

'What do schools achieve that is not accomplished in other ways?' asks Dr Bryan Dockrell, director of the Scottish Council for Research in Education[6]. As regards the acquisition of basic skills, he considers that the research evidence proves conclusively that children who attend school learn more than those who do not. This may well be the case so far as the primary stage is concerned though even here it is possible to point to exceptions to the rule. In Australia children in the outback have been taught to read by radio for many years; in the USA the well-known television programme *Sesame Street* has apparently been more effective than the schools in helping infants to read and to form concepts. And so on. In other words, the evidence is *not* conclusive. Indeed, Dr Dockrell concedes that it might be possible to close the schools with much less social dislocation than is usually supposed, but quotes the findings of the S.C.R.E. publication, *A Study of Fifteen-Year-Olds* which suggest that this is neither practicable nor desirable: 'Those who remained in full-time education made larger gains than those who had attended no classes at all. . . . Those not attending classes have lost some at least of their skills at arithmetic, but the loss in English skills has been only slight'[7].

One might be happier with this assessment if it could be shown that the 'gains' were positively educational, not merely addenda to the sum of cognitive skills already acquired by the learner. Even the most rabid deschoolers do not deny that children learn *something* as a result of going to school: what they are contesting is the implication that learning must always have a measureable content; they believe that some of these allegedly basic skills may soon be irrelevant and in any case may distract attention from more fundamental aspects of learning. Similarly, any gains in measured intelligence attributed to staying on at school – some seven points of IQ between the ages of ten and twenty according to Torsten Husén[8] – must be queried if only because the concept of IQ is itself suspect. As for the 'losses', one is reminded of the truism which tells us that education is what remains when everything that we learned at school has mercifully been forgotten. What counts as a gain on the pedagogical swings may well be a loss on the roundabouts of living.

UNESCO's suppression of Huberman's report which let the cat out of the bag by declaring that 'The idea that the only way people can get education is by being enrolled in institutions is obsolete', is only one example of the official policy of mystification. The plain truth is that the resources and facilities for learning in society at large are immeasurably greater than those available inside schools and colleges. It is only the dog-in-the-manger stance, the institutional habit of clinging to accredited rights and defending them against all comers, that prevents these facilities and resources being fully utilized. Museums, libraries, factories, radio and TV stations, newspaper offices, research institutes, zoos, botanical gardens and a host of other organizations are, potentially at least, resources-for-learning centres whose services might be enlisted – as they are being in the Philadelphia Parkway Plan (the 'school without walls') and in other American cities. The Khrushchev 'Life and work' reforms initiated in the USSR and elsewhere in eastern Europe after 1958 can be seen as a move in the same direction. These reforms, it is true, petered out because the problems of accommodating large numbers on the factory floor or on the collective farm proved to be intractable: things tended to get out of hand when the demonstrator had to cope with hordes of curious observers, or when busloads of eager beavers descended on fields where there was nothing for them to do. It remains to be seen whether the organizational difficulties involved in phasing out compulsory school attendance and getting young people back into circulation in society can be successfully overcome. No one pretends that it is going to be easy. Not everyone agrees that it is necessary. Those who see it as inevitable admit that it is bound to be a slow process. In Philadelphia they have made a modest start involving only a few hundred volunteers, but the numbers are growing and will continue to grow. When Robert Raikes at the end of the eighteenth century launched the Sunday School movement as a means of clearing the streets of ragamuffins and hooligans he initiated an enclosure system (schooling) from which in the course of time grew a powerful superstructure (educational administration) to control it. Two centuries later, the institutional framework is beginning to creak at the hinges. The outside world is bursting in and breaking down the enclosures. Those who are penned inside cannot help but be outward-looking. The machinery originally designed to produce free schools for a 'multitude of laborious poor' now prevents the schools from being free. In short, the contemporary problem is to find ways and means of reversing the train of events which men like Raikes helped to initiate.

In the same way that the Marxist prophecy of the eventual withering away of the state has been falsified, the Marcusian notion that institutional barriers will gradually disappear is certainly over-optimistic. No Joshua trumpetings will bring down the walls of the school overnight. At the same time, it is easier now than it used to be to envisage a situation in which the many agencies within the Knowledge Society could be more effectively mobilized than they are at present. Not only that, but it is becoming clearer how it can be done. The escape route from the trap of the 'hidden curriculum' is the one marked 'extra-curriculum'. This has always been the loophole through which major innovations have edged their way to recognition. It is heartening to recall that many of the 'subjects' whose place in the school's scheme of work is taken for granted – science, modern studies, even English literature – were looked upon as a waste of time by schoolmasters of not so long ago. The indications are that not so long ahead of us, if we exploit the opportunities which are there for the taking – more adventure courses, more adventurous courses – the walls will turn into windows and what we now call a school will be a clearing house, a 'co-ordinating mechanism' as Musgrove calls it. The vision of a learning environment which is as large and as richly stimulating as the learner's lifespace – the world as his oyster – is not after all so impractical.

References

1. F. Musgrove, *Patterns of Power and Responsibility in English Education* (Methuen, 1971), p. 17.
2. Ibid., p. 12.
3. *The Resources Centre, Codsall Comprehensive School* 1971–2 (mimeograph).
4. Herbert Marcuse, *One-Dimensional Man* (RKP, 1964), pp. 152–3.
5. Ted Tapper, *Young People and Society* (Faber, 1971), p. 40.
6. *Research in Education* 7 (Newsletter of the Scottish Council for Research in Education, November 1971).
7. *A Study of Fifteen-Year-Olds*, S.C.R.E. Publications 62 (University of London Press, 1970), pp. 143 and 135.
8. Torsten Husén, 'The influence of schooling on IQ' in Jenkins and Paterson (eds.) *Studies in Individual Differences* (Methuen, 1961).

8 Schooling is geared to the covert objectives of a technological society

The student should not be ashamed to enter into shops and factories, and to ask the craftsman questions and get to know about the details of their work. Formerly men of learning disdained to inquire into these things, which it is of such vital consequence to know and remember. The ignorance grew in succeeding centuries up to the present, so that we know far more about the age of Cicero or of Pliny than about our own grandfathers[1].

So Vives, writing in the first half of the sixteenth century. In the second half of the twentieth, unfortunately, opportunities for free inquiry are rather more restricted. The larger and more powerful the organization, the more closely guarded are its secrets, so that short of the most sophisticated industrial spying there is no way of finding out what it is up to or how it operates. Access to factories, offices, airports, laboratories and other places of work is so strictly limited that the most that can be bargained for is the occasional, officially conducted tour. The progressive division of labour in an advanced industrial society has resulted in the medieval craftsman's 'mystery' becoming a mystery indeed for everyone except the specialist and his employer.

'Look!', 'See for yourself' – there are many learning situations in which these are the only injunctions that are needed. But it is not only exclusion from large-scale organizations which prevents learning in the modern world. Most of the products of high technology are designed to be used and then thrown away so that the purchaser finds it virtually impossible to repair them or to understand how they work. The transistor radio, the outboard motor, power steering and automatic gear changing in automobiles, central heating in the home – these are only some of the devices which not only keep us dependent on the expertise of technicians but minimize our capacity for self-help. Opportunities for learning by example, too, are increasingly in short supply. Of all the insidious effects of institutionalized schooling, two of the most potent are the widespread conviction that education is only obtainable on the terms offered by those who control the system, and that the learner, of necessity, must rely on others to do things which formerly he was able to do for himself.

For most widely shared skills, a person who demonstrates the skill is the only human resource we ever need or get [says Illich]. Whether in speaking or driving, in cooking or in the use of communication equipment, we are often barely conscious of formal instruction and learning, especially after our first experience of the materials in question. I see no reason why other complex skills, such as the mechanical aspects of surgery* and playing the fiddle, of reading or the use of directories and catalogues, could not be learned in the same way.

A well-motivated student who does not labour under a specific handicap often needs no further assistance than can be provided by someone who can demonstrate on demand how to do what the learner wants to learn to do. The demand made of skilled people that before demonstrating their skill they be certified as pedagogues is a result of the insistence either that people learn what they do not want to know or that all people – even those with a special handicap – learn certain things, at a given moment in their lives, and preferably under specified circumstances[2].

---

* 'Rather him than me as a patient of such a surgeon' is the obvious comment here!

Anyone who doubts this, and members of the teaching profession will be the first to resent it as an attack on their prerogatives, has only to look around him to see how true it is: motorways thronged with drivers who never attended an autoschool, dance halls crowded with singers and instrumentalists who never had a music lesson in their lives, flats decorated and dinners prepared by people who never went near a course of homecraft or domestic science. Those who protest that the deschoolers are simply anarchists and iconoclasts who have nothing to offer in the way of viable alternatives to the existing system might do worse than consider the merits of Illich's proposal for a network of easily accessible resources for informal learning. These proposals are nothing if not realistic. They include:

(1) Reference services – drawing up an inventory of 'educational objects' (including those in use in industry and commerce as well as those housed in museums, libraries and art galleries) which can be made available to students.
(2) Skill exchanges – listing the names and addresses of all persons who are willing to serve as skill models and demonstrators.
(3) Peer matching – to enable persons with a common interest to get together and pursue it further.
(4) Professional consultants – a directory of experienced educators whose function would be to provide advice and leadership for parents and students as and when these were required.

A computerized 'learning web' of this sort need not be relegated to the realms of science fiction for it already exists in places albeit incipiently. Extramural courses based on universities provide one obvious example. If the plan were to be implemented it would enable any individual, for a small subscription charge, to dial for the education services of his choice as and when he wished in much the same way he now uses the telephone service. At a stroke, this would bring into being the kind of institution which Illich styles as 'convivial', though it is easy to see that such a system might be abused or even 'bugged' by unscrupulous eavesdroppers and line-tapping agencies. (So what? Why worry?) Conceivably, too, the work of co-ordinating and running such a network might

give rise to an administrative superstructure very like the bureaucracy we now have. Nevertheless, it would go far to change the
present relationship between a take-it-or-leave-it supplier and a
consumer whose 'needs' are decided for him whether he likes it or
not.

Plans for giving the learner more of a say in deciding his own
destiny run counter to those of an education system which is at
once the servant and slave of the wider system of a technological
society. Roszak notes that:

> We are bitterly familiar with totalitarian politics in the form of
> brutal regimes which achieve their integration by bludgeon and
> bayonet. But in the case of a technocracy, totalitarianism is
> perfected because its techniques become progressively more
> subliminal. The distinctive feature of the regime of experts lies
> in the fact that, while possessing ample power to coerce, it
> prefers to charm conformity from us by exploiting our deep-
> seated commitment to the scientific world view and by mani-
> pulating the securities and creature comforts of the industrial
> affluence which science has given us.
>
> So subtle and so well-rationalized have the arts of technocratic
> domination become in our advanced industrial societies that
> even those in the state and/or corporate structure who dominate
> our lives must find it impossible to conceive of themselves as
> the agents of a totalitarian control. Rather, they easily see them-
> selves as the conscientious managers of a munificent social
> system which is, by the very fact of its broadcast affluence,
> incompatible with any form of exploitation[3].

Unconscious and well-meaning as it usually is, this is indeed the
logic of domination. Neo-Freudians like Marcuse and Norman
Brown have sought to plumb its psychological origins and have
found themselves in deep waters as a consequence. Without
presuming to emulate them, it seems that what is involved here is
nothing less than a flaw in the human condition. Marcuse calls it
'surplus repression'. Whatever name we choose for it, it springs
from the incorrigible urge of the strong to mastermind the weak.
At the conscious level it manifests itself in a theory and practice of
education which is, as we say, teacher-centred; more crudely, the
kind of education which sees nothing wrong in one person taking
charge of another's ego. On these terms, the relationship between

teacher and taught is not one of mutual give-and-take, a partnership between equals as it is with friends and lovers: rather, it assumes the right to do things *to, with,* and *for* the other. At worst, the domination is a form of psychological rape: at best, a seduction.

The ways in which schooling induces standardization are plainer to see than they were. J. S. Mill's essay *On Liberty* (1859) contains truths which have been slow in coming home to us, notably his resounding denunciation of state-controlled education as 'a mere contrivance for moulding people to be exactly like one another'. Unaware as we are of the unobtrusive side-effects of schooling, we are all disinclined to believe that anything like this can possibly have happened to *us*. (Rats in a Skinner box are no less oblivious.) The fact that it *has* happened can be illustrated in a number of ways. Frank Musgrove instances one of the neatest:

> The camera has provided us with vivid visual evidence of the rapid process of standardization in the closing decades of the nineteenth century. In 1912 Arthur Ponsonby considered that the public schools were turning out a stereotyped product, in sharp contrast to forty or fifty years previously. Organized, compulsory games (bitterly opposed by Moberly at Winchester, and by other headmasters who were correctly reading the signs of the times), were now as general as the school certificate examinations. Ponsonby pointed to the variety of attire and posture in photographs of mid nineteenth-century football teams: boys were 'lounging about in different attitudes with a curious variety of costumes'. But by 1912:
>> The group of today consists of two or three rows of boys beautifully turned out with immaculate, perfectly fitting clothing. . . . They stand and sit so that the line of the peaks of their caps, of the folded hands and their bare knees, is mathematically level. And even their faces! You can hardly tell one from another[4].

The indications are that contemporary youth culture may mark a turning point.

By this time the exasperated reader is doubtless thinking that these repeated attempts to draw attention to the unseen side-effects of schooling rely on the kind of trick first performed by McLuhan in *The Medium is the Message,* and that they deserve no better than to be dismissed as a Reds-under-the-bed fallacy. Can nothing be taken at its face value, it may be asked? Seeing that schools existed since the days of the Sumerians why should we be greatly concerned about the alleged vices of the hidden curriculum today?

The answer comes pat. Until recent times schooling for the masses had very limited objectives, summarized in the nineteenth century as the 3 Rs: it was not conceived as an all-purpose enterprise controlled by outfitters who undertook to turn out a finished product. Socialization was a natural process, not one confined to the school premises. The techniques of persuasion and coercion at the school's disposal were nothing like so consummate as they are today.

There is nothing wrong in telling a boy that he has got 6 out of 10 for arithmetic: there is everything wrong in telling him that he has got 6 out of 10 for life. If body counts are obscene, mind counts are worse. Yet it is not only psychometry which is based on E. L. Thorndike's proposition that 'Whatever is exists in some amount': the entire ethos of the education system is predicated upon it. From start to finish, modern schooling stands for the belief that each and every aspect of human worth and endeavour can be measured. If it is cynical to say that every man has his price, it is certainly not cynical to say that as the education system thinks of him, every schoolchild can be graded, docketed and slotted into his appropriate place on the assembly line. Whether we take the factory or the office block as our model for the school the analogy is close enough. It is not simply that the planners are increasingly driven to thinking in terms of input-output analysis, cost effectiveness and optimization of efficiency: inevitably, pupils also learn to think of themselves in similar terms. As raw material for processing they are constantly being subjected to quality controls. Intelligence tests, personality tests, aptitude tests, attitude scales, achievement tests, end-of-term examinations, continuous assessment – one by one the dipsticks are inserted and the clinical measurements recorded as scores, quotients, percentages, correlations, marks, rank orders, points on a scale, ratings, classes. Evaluation is all one with mensuration in the accountancy of educational research. Nothing is left out of the reckoning except, of course, the learner's identity.

It is only fair to add that those who make and administer mental tests are suitably cautious in the claims made for their validity and reliability. It is only within recent years that the popular myth of the 'constancy of the IQ' has been exploded. The trouble is that although psychologists and educationists are often at pains to explain that the measuring rods they use are blunt instruments, and that the greatest care must be taken in interpreting the 'results', the person being tested tends to accept them implicitly. Because he does not 'know the score', what else can he do when he finds (as he often does) that his intelligence has been totted up as 95 points and that after filling in what looked like a perfectly innocent questionnaire his personality has been entered in his record card as unstable. The damage is done. It cannot easily be explained away.

> People who have been schooled down to size let immeasured experience slip out of their hands. To them, what cannot be measured becomes secondary, threatening. They do not have to be robbed of their creativity. Under instruction, they have unlearned to 'do' their thing or 'be' themselves, and value only what has been made or could be made.
>
> Once people have the idea schooled into them that values can be produced and measured, they tend to accept all kinds of rankings. There is a scale for the development of nations, another for the intelligence of babies, and even progress towards peace can be calculated according to body count. In a schooled world the road to happiness is paved with a consumer's index[5].

When asked why he goes to school, the academically inclined pupil's reply more often than not is, 'in order to pass examinations'. When asked why he does not share the same ambition, the non-academic pupil's answer is equally blinkered, 'because I'm not clever'. While schooling may afford outlets for creativity, in general it fosters convergent frames of mind. What little we know about genuine creativity – and when all the findings from the enormous research literature in this hazy field have been sifted it is little enough – tells us that the diverger is likely to be recognized in the classroom only as an obnoxious individual, a nuisance whose presence interferes with the smooth running of the teacher's normal routine. This is why men of distinction, even genius, were often assigned relatively low IQs at school. This is why public examinations, no matter how hard they try to make allowances for originality and critical judgement, favour the candidate who plays safe and regurgitates the information and ideas that have been fed to him during the prescribed course. To step out of line, he knows, is too risky: the 'right' answers, in literature as in mathematics, are the ones approved by his examiners.

In this way, learning in all its 57 varieties is programmed in a pre-established pattern. If he wants to better himself, to be *anybody*, the learner has to spend more and more of his time being fitted out for the expedition of life in the crowded local branch of a chain store whose empire never ceases to expand. Optimization of the system means optimization of the self. Whatever else he learns or fails to learn, the euphoric state of mind which flatters itself that every day and in every way things are getting better and better is inescapable.

Or is it? As always, the poet's estimation is wiser than the pundit's. The school that is made of marble may be a *superpallazzo* but e. e. cummings might agree with the Newsom boy in dismissing it as 'an incredibly vulgar detention camp swarming with every conceivable species of undesirable organism'. It takes the perception of the child to outwit the sophistries of the adult, to see that education with a capital E

> is a 9 letter word
> used by inferior magicians
> with the wrong alchemical formula for transforming
>   earth into gold
> funky warlocks operating on guesswork[6].

References

1. Quoted in W. Boyd, *A History of Western Education*, 9th ed. (Black, 1969), p. 181.
2. Ivan Illich, *Deschooling Society* (Calder & Boyars, 1971), p. 88.
3. Theodore Roszak, *The Making of a Counter Culture* (Faber, 1969), p. 9.
4. F. Musgrove, *Patterns of Power and Responsibility in English Education* (Methuen, 1971), pp. 139–40.
5. Ivan Illich, *Deschooling Society*, p. 40.
6. Allen Ginsberg, 'Wichita Vortex Sutra' in *Planet News 1961–67* (McBride and Broadley, 1968).

9 Schooling creates an artificial demand for more schooling

Like Hamlet, we 'eat the air, promise-crammed'. The rapid expansion of the educational services is part and parcel of the drive for economic growth; it arises from the same motives and follows the same course. The reasons for thinking that excessive importance is attached to schooling are identical with those adduced by economists who rail against the crass worship of productivity. Galbraith for one:

> Its importance is buttressed by a highly dubious but widely accepted psychology of want; by an equally dubious but equally accepted interpretation of national interest; and by powerful vested interest. So all-embracing, indeed, is our sense of the importance of production as a goal that the first reaction to any questioning of this attitude will be, 'What else is there?' So large does production bulk in our thoughts that we can only suppose that a vacuum must remain if it should be relegated to a lesser role[1].

In a schooled society the tendency is for rates of consumption of schooling to increase indefinitely as if there were no limits to growth. Not the felt need, but the fear that he may be missing something which the conventional wisdom urges upon him, spurs the individual consumer. 'One man's consumption becomes his neighbour's wish. This already means that the process by which wants are satisfied is also the process by which wants are created. The more wants are satisfied, the more new ones are born. . . '[2]. Thus, the schooled man, like the diabetic, must keep up his doses or die.

Unfortunately, Galbraith himself compounds the problem. On the one hand, he contends that an educational policy based on investment in human capital suffers from the same defects, and has the same consequences, as investment in material production: on the other, he approves whole-heartedly of education as a consumer good. So far as he can see, the only exit from the squirrel's cage is by entry into the new class – the salaried professionals who enjoy the work they are doing for its own sake, or at least rate job satisfaction higher than a big pay packet. The trouble is, of course, that this happy release from routine repetitive labour is only possible for those who have acquired the necessary formal qualifications, and these, with few exceptions, are only obtainable after a lengthy period of schooling.

How to relegate schooling to a lesser role? How to de-emphasize its obsessive influence? As the necessity to 'earn a living' diminishes – and already the nineteenth century's industrial work ethic is visibly eroded – answers to these questions will be easier than they are at present. As things are, it is not too difficult to anticipate the form the answers will take. It needs no philosopher king to explain to the inhabitants of the cave that the shadows they see before them are not the genuine stuff of education. It needs no expert economist to show that the money spent on raising the school-leaving age to sixteen is unlikely to bring about any significant rise in formal attainment among the majority of pupils. Quite apart from its likely counterproductive effects in bringing to a head the latent frustration and resentment of teenagers, the cost-benefit aspects of this latest extension of the school life are extremely dubious.

Suppose, for the sake of argument, the school-leaving age were to be lowered to thirteen with the proviso that all pupils were required to attain minimal levels of proficiency in literacy and numeracy, or stay on until they did, and that thereafter attendance at the secondary stage would become optional. Can it honestly be said that putting an end to compulsion would leave most adolescents any worse off than they are at present? Who is to say that any risk of loss in cognitive skills would not be offset by the inestimable gains in personal freedom?

References

1. J. K. Galbraith, *The Affluent Society* (Hamish Hamilton, 1958), p. 91.
2. Ibid., p. 120.

10 Schooling splits society into factions

Recently there's been a storm kicked up by parents of students at the Strand Grammar School, Brixton, who complain that their children are terrorized by pupils of Tulse Hill Comprehensive School. Parents say their boys are being beaten up, robbed and 'wind up in the casualty wards of hospitals'. One father said his son was kicked so hard 'he spent eight days in hospital and almost lost the sight of one eye'. (No, this wasn't in Harlem, it was in dear old law-abiding London.) One father put his finger on the heart of things by saying, 'They regard it as part of their lives and accept it'[1].

It would be wrong to suppose that this state of affairs arises solely from the friction caused by the side-by-side existence of selective and non-selective types of secondary school. The Tulse Hill–Strand confrontation may be taken as a paradigm of the education system as a whole. Lacey's model (Fig. 1), elaborated in his study of Hightown Grammar, shows how differentiation inevitably brings about polarization in a selective secondary school even among pupils from roughly the same social background. By *differentiation* he means 'the separation and ranking of students according to a multiple set of criteria which makes up the normative, academically orientated, value system of the grammar school'. *Polarization* he defines as 'a process of subculture formation in which the school-dominated, normative culture is opposed by an alternative culture which I refer to as the "anti-group" culture'[2].

What happens is only too familiar. The intake of 11-year-olds is made up of boys fresh from primary schools in which they figured as the 'best pupils', proud of their new caps and blazers, eager beavers who are only too willing to do their best. As a homogeneous ability group they are assigned at random to four classes, follow the same kind of course and are taught by the same kind of teachers. At the end of the first year the group is split up on the basis of examination results, the top percentiles being creamed off to form an 'express' stream (which is forthwith taken over by 'crack' teachers and groomed for O- and A-levels), while the rest are classified as 2A, 2B and 2C (and relegated to the limbo of lost

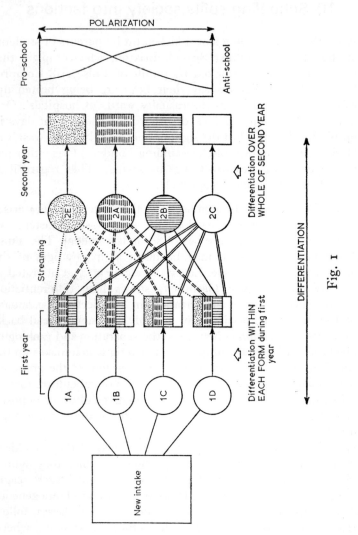

Fig. I

causes). Within two years the effects of this differential treatment
are quite startlingly evident: at one extreme (2E) a group of well-
behaved boys whose allegiance to the school and all it stands for is
never in question, at the other (2C) a deliquescent group characterized by sullen apathy and ill-disguised hostility.

The stresses and strains involved in the process of differentiation
are as easily exaggerated as they are easily glossed over; Lacey
mentions truancy, sleeplessness, bed-wetting, feeling sick and
bursting into tears as frequent symptoms – which could perhaps
be described as mildly neurotic. The fact that a great many
children are not unduly affected and seem to take to schooling like
ducks to water is neither here nor there: the point is that what
happens within the confines of the grammar school is typical of the
system as a whole.

The case of identical twins who happen to be placed above and
below the borderline in the 11-plus examination and who are
accordingly allocated to different types of secondary school is no
less revealing. Coming from the same home, they soon develop
markedly distinct life-styles, mix with peer groups whose interests
and aspirations – popular culture and high culture, non-academic
and academic – have little in common. Blood is thicker than water,
to be sure, but schooling has its own ways of weakening family
ties. Especially where working-class children are changing their
social status, mother and daughter, father and son, sister and
brother often do not see eye to eye with each other. Many a sixth
former is secretly ashamed of his parents. Without actually dis-
owning them, he finds that his tastes in reading, his choice of radio
and television programmes, his topics of intelligent conversation
are somehow estranged from theirs. Many an undergraduate,
similarly, feels a furtive sense of guilt at stepping out of his class.
Many a happy home becomes slightly uncomfortable, even if it
avoids open strife, as sooner rather than later one or more of its
members moves into a new and different world from that of his
family.

In the USSR fears that the provision of mass education might
result in the formation of an intelligentsia separated from the
proletariat have been expressed off and on since the days of Lenin.
Hindsight shows that they have not prevented the emergence of an
élite class and that the causes of alienation are not simply economic
as Marx thought. Historically, these causes can be traced back to

the medieval distinction between the cleric and the illiterate. In other words, their origins are to be found in the schooling process itself. In modern times this separation of different kinds of knowledge and learning has given rise to a host of subtle class distinctions. Sir Peter Venables' 'grammar' reminds us:

> I am resolute; thou art firm; he is *obstinate*
> I am pure; thou art applied; he is *technological*
> I educate; you teach; he *trains*

Schooling emphasizes the relatively minor differences in certain kinds of cognitive abilities at the expense of ignoring those major attributes which give human life its meaning and dignity. By discounting practical (or 'profane') knowledge and by placing a heavy premium on scholastic values, it instils the belief that the only possible aim in life is to surpass others in academic achievement. On these terms, as Illich says, education becomes worldly and the world becomes non-educational.

So higher education plumes itself on being a cut above further education: so the university looks askance at the polytechnic, Oxbridge at Redbrick, the honours graduate at the ordinary degree man, the academic secondary pupil at the non-academic, the middle class at the working class. Differentiation is of the essence in schooling.

In the nineteenth century the split level between the provision of elementary schools for the plebs and public schools for the ruling aristocracy found its obvious political expression in the Two Nations. In the twentieth the policy of divide and rule has been carried a good deal further than this. Not only are selective and non-selective secondary schools permitted to exist side by side (on the understanding that oil and water cannot mix), but also a dual system exists of 'sponsored mobility' for the few and of 'contest mobility' for the many. According to R. H. Turner, social mobility is only maintained 'by training the masses to regard themselves as relatively incompetent to manage society, by restricting access to the skills and manners of the élite, and by cultivating belief in the superior competence of the élite'[3].

In practice this political theory is implemented by schooling.

Certainly, Litt's examination of civics textbooks and programmes used in schools in the Boston area with different socio-economic groups revealed that their contents seemed deliberately designed to reinforce the differential political orientations of those groups:

Students in the different communities are being trained to play different political roles and to respond to political phenomena in different ways. In the working-class community, where political involvement is low, the arena of civic education offers training in the basic democratic procedures without stressing political participation or the citizen's view of conflict and dis-agreement as indigenous to the political system. Only in the affluent and politically vibrant community (Alpha) are insights into political processes and functions of politics passed on to those who, judging from their socio-economic and political environment, will likely man those positions that involve them in influencing or making political decisions. (p. 492).

Similarly, from his study of the socialization of British secondary school students, Abramson suspected that, like the Boston children, 'British children in non-selective schools are taught to accept relatively non-participatory roles in the political system', whilst 'teachers assume that public schoolboys and grammar school sixth formers may attain leadership roles in the society and the polity'[4].

However naïve it may be to represent schooling as a device for separating the haves from the havenots there can be little doubt that the wholesale expansion of the educational services has been largely motivated by *envy*. The picture of a neighbourhood divided against itself as presented by the parents and pupils of Tulse Hill Comprehensive and Strand Grammar School merely mirrors in a small way an international scene composed of self-styled developed and underdeveloped nations. Everywhere it is the same story. By decreeing that the only knowledge that is of any worth must be institutionally sanctioned, schooling creates the impression that it is indispensable and that no alternative is possible. As the opiate of the people it is highly successful. It has its own methods of dealing with the few who refuse to be hooked (like those wretches in 2C): either it earmarks them for remedial treatment or simply leaves them to stew in their own juice. Like all totalitarian regimes, schooling begins by overruling organized opposition and ends by making opposition all but impossible.

References
1. The *Observer*, 5 December 1971.
2. C. Lacey, *Hightown Grammar* (Manchester University Press, 1970), p. 57.
3. R. H. Turner, 'Modes of social ascent through education: sponsored and contest mobility' in A. H. Halsey, J. Floud and C. A. Anderson (eds.), *Education, Economy and Society* (New York Free Press, 1961).
4. H. Entwistle, *Political Education in a Democracy* (RKP, 1971), pp. 14–15.

11 Schooling stands in the way of liberal education so long as it remains compulsory

Tom Sawyer never read *Emile* and would not have made much of it if he had tried: for all that, he had a shrewd appreciation, when it came to whitewashing, of the distinction which Rousseau drew between *labor* and *opus*. Ski-ing and show jumping can be trying and dangerous pastimes, but for those who indulge in them there is no hardship in joining ski schools and riding schools and submitting themselves to courses of instruction. Schools of this sort answer to Illich's description of 'convivial' institutions. If everyone were to be coerced into joining them it would be a different story.

The run-of-the-mill school is emphatically *not* a convivial institution. The inference is that it could easily become one if it were free from compulsory attendance. Philosophers may debate the rights and wrongs of 'freedom-for' and 'freedom-from', but in the final analysis what matters is the sense, however illusory, of 'feeling free'. The volunteer and the conscript who join the Army, Navy, or the Air Force both become members of the same organization and are bound by the same regulations. The fact that one enjoys the experience of being subjected to military discipline and the other hates it may have little to do with the nature of the organization or its regulations. One difference arises from the *conditions of entry*. It is the difference between being invited and ordered to engage in an activity.

Why is it that after the age of thirteen or fourteen many pupils find the necessity of attending school irksome? At the primary stage there is often no trace of resentment and the atmosphere of many of the schools might well be described as convivial. What happens in the developmental psychology of teenagers, particularly those who are not academically inclined, to bring about this change from *opus* to *labor*?

There is plenty of evidence to show that organized schooling has progressively encroached on the personal responsibility of children during the last 100 years. Apart from having to present himself at meals, morning prayers, classes and the evening roll call, the early Victorian schoolboy's time was his own and he was allowed to use it as he pleased. His private life was left severely alone by the headmaster and his staff, whose chief concern was with the formal curriculum – Latin and Greek. This is not to say that his privacy was respected by his fellow inmates, for discipline was largely left to the boys themselves, with the result that the younger ones were frequently tyrannized and subjected to all manner of petty indignities (and not so petty abuses). No matter, for sensitive souls like Shelley there were always corners to weep in; for sturdier lads, roaming the countryside alone or with friends, bird-nesting, fishing, poaching and other pursuits offered avenues of escape, or at least respite from the tedium of Livy and Ovid. Informally organized common-interest groups (later to be canonized as 'extra-curricular activities') flourished. At Eton there was a longstanding tradition by which young bloods and sprigs of nobility promoted public race meetings: at Rugby they kept their own pack of foxhounds. It was all free and easy, and no doubt very untidy. The irony of it all is that, in their old-fashioned, permissive way, these schools incorporated many of the features which have since been designated as 'progressive'.

After 1870 all this changed, thanks to what Bamford calls 'a subtle but organized drive by authority to sublimate the boy's self to a team. . . . The old principle of respecting a boy's character and allowing it to develop in private gave way to a regulated existence, with the boy's leisure ruthlessly timetabled and supervised'[1].

Left to themselves, many boys revel in taking part in organized games. The miseries inflicted by compulsory games in English public schools – significantly, a development dating from the period of the first Education Acts – have been eloquently documented in many an autobiography, but the overall undesirable effects of compulsion have received rather less notice.

Boys had always played to win – Tom Brown is sufficient
evidence of that – but in the early years it was a glorious
extempore achievement. Later, winning became a serious preoccupation, even for many masters, and for many of the boys
the only thing about the school that mattered. A feverish fight
developed for perfection in muscular activity, the desire to win
going hand in hand with a nonchalant superficial air of not
caring about the result. The ideal became not only a complete
concealment of the emotions, but the masking of them with a
false facade, i.e. the stiff upper lip. This was the new manliness,
extolled as such. It amounted to a changeover from the loosely
governed, emotionally enthusiastic and romping play to the
serious professional approach under the eye of expert coaches.
The pressure was for greater and greater skills producing more
and more glorious results, until the time given it outstripped the
simple ideas of playing the game as a game[2].

If, instead of the playing-field context, one thinks of the classroom, the above passage reads very like a summary of developments in state schooling since its inception in 1870. There, too, it
was a case of 'the serious professional approach under the eye of
expert coaches'; there, too, 'the pressure was for greater and
greater skills producing more and more glorious results': there,
too, winning became the main preoccupation and romping play
was frowned on and driven out of bounds. The controls over the
learner's life grew steadily tighter and more restrictive. Today, in
the more enlightened public schools the rules governing organized
games have either been relaxed or abandoned altogether because
they are seen to subvert, if not to defeat, their own purposes.
A similar relaxation in the rules governing school attendance
may be anticipated, if it is not already overdue. If compulsion
has been found to be undesirable in one context, why not in
another?
     Legal compulsion for all beyond the age of twelve is a twentieth-
century phenomenon. The aim of the 1870 Education Act was a
limited one, 'to fill up the gaps' left by the various voluntary agencies.
It is interesting to reflect that even at the time the reasons for
thinking that legal compulsion was necessary were confused. In his
essay on *A Liberal Education; and Where to Find it* (1868), Thomas
Huxley commented on the diversity of opinion which made this

issue so controversial and left his readers in no doubt that his own
position was, to say the least, sceptical:

> We English, in spite of constant experience to the contrary,
> preserve a touching faith in the efficacy of Acts of Parliament;
> and I believe we should have compulsory education in the
> course of next session, if there were the least probability that
> half a dozen leading statesmen of different parties would agree
> what that education should be.
>
> Some hold that education without theology is worse than
> none. Others maintain quite as strongly that education with
> theology is in the same predicament. But this is certain, those
> who hold the first opinion can by no means agree what theology
> should be taught; and that those who maintain the second are
> in a small minority.
>
> At any rate 'make people learn to read, write and cipher' say a
> great many; and the advice is undoubtedly sensible as far as it
> goes. But, as has happened to me in former days, those who, in
> despair of getting anything better, advocate this measure, are
> met with the objection that it is very like making a child practise
> the use of knife, fork, and spoon without giving it a particle of
> meat. I really don't know what reply is to be made to such an
> objection.

Neither do we, for all the stress we put on the importance of the
basic skills. Huxley, at least, never made the mistake of equating
schooling with education: indeed, from what he says, he was not
even sure that the one was a necessary precondition for the other.

> Suppose that an adult man, in the full vigour of his faculties,
> could be suddenly placed in the world, as Adam is said to have
> been, and then left to do as he might. How long would he be left
> uneducated? Not five minutes. Nature would begin to teach
> him, through the eye, the ear, the touch, the properties of
> objects.
>
> Education is the instruction of the intellect in the laws of
> Nature, under which name I include not merely things and their
> forces, but men and their ways; and the fashioning of the
> affections and of the will into an earnest and loving desire to
> move in harmony with those laws. For me, education means
> neither more nor less than this. Anything which professes to

call itself education must be tried by this standard, and if it fails to stand the test I will not call it education, whatever may be the force of authority, or of numbers, on the other side[3].

The force of authority, needless to say, took a different line. From the start, the reasons for thinking that compulsion was necessary stemmed from an extraordinarily explosive mixture of religious, economic and political motives in which the educational ingredient was minor and incidental.

In the course of time the religious motive has lost its force. Indeed, one of the strongest arguments against compulsion in any shape or form is to be found in the counterproductive effect of the clauses in the 1944 Education Act requiring a daily act of corporate worship and religious instruction in all schools in England and Wales. If we agree with Mager in thinking that the supreme objective in any course of instruction is to leave the student at least as favourably disposed to the subject at the end of the day as he was at the beginning, then the experience of twenty-five years and more of compulsory religious instruction provides a sorry demonstration of the wrong way to go about it.

The decline of religion has left the field open to political and economic motives. University education, once the home and haven of liberal studies, has become increasingly biased in the direction of professional training. Further education, more often than not, is another word for vocational training. As for the secondary schools, at any rate so far as their non-certificate courses are concerned, most of what passes under the name of general education might be referred to more appropriately as socialization. In other words, the doubts expressed by Huxley have been justified: 100 years of state-controlled schooling have certainly failed to stand the test set by him.

Once instituted, schooling took on a life of its own, establishing its own arbitrary standards, its own norms of behaviour, its self-contained culture. As Shipman says, 'The complex, differentiated nature of industrial societies applies to values as well as organization. Religion, philosophy, science, education and communication tend to separate as distinct institutions rather than being bound together in the same comprehensive framework of custom. The value, paramount to each tend to be distinctive and to become increasingly autonomous'[4].

This assumption of autonomy needs to be resisted. So long as schooling was limited to the three Rs and little else, so long as it was relatively short in duration and had the backing of religious orthodoxy, there was little harm in compulsion. Its conveyor-belt procedures, threadbare curriculum and barrack-square methods could be excused on the grounds of scarcity of resources, large numbers or the shortage of teachers. No one pretended that it was any better than it was. Unfortunately because this is how the system works in practice, the tendency increasingly is to rationalize it in a theory which is essentially mechanical. As a selective agency the school holds a key position in the promotion of social mobility and the maintenance of social stability: hence, say the theorists, its function is to grade pupils and train them for different roles. 'School prepares them for their future in a world of organization and bureaucracy.' Just how it is able to do this, or entitled to try, seeing that it is largely closed off from that world is a question that the powers-that-be rarely care to ask. It might be thought that so long as pupils are confined to an institution which proclaims its separate identity the less chance they will have of finding their feet outside it. Modern educational theory arrogates the right to make crucial decisions affecting the learner's life at all points and in all its dimensions. It is based on the need for prediction and control. Skinner and his kind are not alone in believing that the learner can be treated as an organism whose behaviour is sufficiently law-abiding for the teacher-programmer-manager to be able to make reliable forecasts about what it will do. According to this view, the child is not born a living soul but rather a product to be machined, conceived of first and foremost as a recipient, not an agent, a creature for processing, not a creator. 'If a man is to be produced it is necessary that he be formed by education.' The seed planted by Comenius at the dawn of the modern era has sprouted into a many-branching tree in which 'the sacred and hidden identity which no techniques can reach' has almost disappeared from sight.

Tom Sawyer, that ace of truants, knew better. So do the Liverpudlian youngsters (and their parents) who are respond-ing whole-heartedly to the breakaway movement begun by the Scotland Road Community Trust. It is a sad commentary on the low level to which official educational policy has been reduced that the only working definition of a free school we appear to be left with is one which does not charge for admission. To be truly free,

D

the school needs to satisfy far more hospitable conditions of entry than this. As a meeting place, it must be open to all comers and at all hours, a centre where anyone can drop in at odd times, a good place to come in out of the cold. Attendance looks after itself in a learning community where the supply and demand for education are allowed to float. No one stays away when all are accepted as responsible agents. Associate members are glad to participate in a going concern because there is never any suggestion that they need to undergo a process of corrective treatment.

As applied in the past, legal compulsion may have served a useful purpose. In a less servile society, its retention is as anachronistic as that of corporal punishment. Until the education system is rid of it, schooling cannot be other than illiberal.

References

1. T. W. Bamford, *The Rise of the Public Schools* (Nelson, 1967), p. 79.
2. Ibid., p. 57.
3. Cf. C. Bibby (ed.), *Thomas Huxley on Education* (Cambridge University Press, 1971), pp. 66–7.
4. M. Shipman, *Education and Modernization* (Faber, 1971), p. 18.

Section III

THE CHANGING SCHOOL

THE CHANGING SCHOOL

From an archaeological point of view, schools are as old as Babylon. What is reputed to be the earliest classroom yet excavated, the Tablet House at Mari in Mesopotamia, has been estimated to date from about 2000 BC. From the dawn of civilization writing and reckoning were invested with magical, mystic significance and closely associated with the priesthood. According to one authority:

Evidence from a number of documents of the Third Dynasty of Ur shows that scribes were drawn generally from the more influential social classes; this represents, possibly, some hardening of class barriers with literacy becoming indicative of social superiority. Whether girls could become scribes is not certain; there is, however, a little evidence to suggest that some did. All scribes had to specialize in one branch of the bureaucracy – the temple, law, medicine, commerce, the army, or teaching itself – and underwent, in consequence, two periods of training. The first, in basic literacy, was given by group instruction; this was followed by appointment to the particular government department where higher and more specialized instruction was obtained through a system of apprenticeship and individual tuition[1].

It would appear from this that schooling from the start was identified with the inculcation of basic literacy (with the emphasis on *writing*), and that it was organized on bureaucratic lines. (Or could it be that archaeologists interpret the remains of Sumerian civilization in this way because they are influenced by the modern concept of schooling?) However this may be, the circumstances under which the modern, state-controlled system operates differ from those of all previous ages in at least three important respects.

In the first place, schooling in earlier times was limited in its scope and objectives. In the second, it was not provided for all children (as it was not then considered an essential medium for enculturation). Thirdly, the resources needed for the maintenance of schools were within the reach of individuals and local community groups. None of these conditions holds good in the contemporary situation, and the prevailing view seems to be that they cannot be satisfied in an advanced industrial society. Be this as it may, each of them has far-reaching implications which need to be discussed in turn.

1 The objectives of schooling

The Greek word for 'school' provides as good a starting point for discussion as any: it was synonymous with leisure. Latinized as *ludus* (a game), its etymology bears witness to the fact that schooling was originally thought of as being of marginal importance, and functioning, if at all, on an informal, take-it-or-leave-it basis. In *The Republic* and elsewhere in the *Dialogues*, Plato makes it plain that some parents thought it advisable to send their boys to the music master (*kitharistes*) and the athletics coach (*paidotribes*), while others preferred to bring them up at home. Custom rather than the law charged the father with the moral duty of training his sons in the rudimentary skills ('Music for the soul, gymnastics for the body') which were indispensable for active membership in the corporate life. It was not until the music master's work began to include training children to read and write and a new species of teacher, the *grammatistes*, appeared that a less easygoing attitude gained ground. Protagoras is represented as saying that, 'Those who can best afford this kind of instruction spend most upon it: their sons go earliest to school and leave the latest'.

Schooling served a purely propaedeutic purpose. As such, it played a relatively unimportant part in the growing-up process. Its curriculum was of the simplest. The Athenian can scarcely be accused of undervaluing literacy; numerous public inscriptions as well as frequent references to literacy in the works of their dramatists are evidence that most Athenians could read.* But any idea that this accomplishment necessitated attendance at school would have struck them as preposterous – though not so preposterous as the idea that attendance at school was the best and only way to become educated. Learning to read, apparently, was as natural and as easy as learning to wrestle or throw the javelin.

In the heyday of the city state, schooling was neither formalized nor compulsory. In practice, there were no schools in the modern sense, only teachers who offered their services as demonstrators of certain skills.

If we look for a point in time when schooling began to assume the formal institutionalized aspect it has now we shall find it somewhere in the sixteenth century. Not that Renaissance ideas of compulsory schooling or nationwide education systems were immediately implemented. It was left to the Protestant thinkers of the Reformation to do that. 'Erasmus laid the egg which Luther hatched,' as the historical cliché puts it.

The step which Luther dared to take involved the reversal of the 1,000-year-old doctrine that 'We believe in order to know'. For Luther knowledge came before faith. He asserted the right and duty of the individual to judge for himself, to demand empirical proof, and like Descartes later, to accept nothing as true that it is possible to doubt. The Reformation upheaval provided the motive force behind the early proposals for mass education. All the Reformation planners – Luther, Calvin, Knox, Comenius, Milton and Dury – saw education as a means of exercising power over people. 'If a man is to be produced it is necessary that he be formed by education,' Comenius declared. For Milton, the aim was 'to repair the ruins of our first parents'; for Dury, 'to lead men captive under the yoke of Christ'.

* For the evidence of widespread public literacy in Athens in the fifth and sixth centuries BC see J. Bowen. *A History of Western Education*, vol. I (Methuen, 1972), p. 74 *et seq.*

But the Protestant ethic was a two-edged sword. Seen from one side, it entitled each individual to judge the evidence of Holy Writ for himself, hence the need for universal literacy. Seen from the other, it upheld the claims of a new kind of manmade authority – education – to shape men's lives for them. A theory which set its sights no lower than the saving of souls prompted the search (which is still going on) for a methodology as certain in its operation and results as that of the scientist's. Instead of being an adjunct to the child's life, schooling was to be its entire business.

In the event, these Protestant schemes for establishing national education systems had to wait another 200 years and more before they were implemented, by which time the needs of an industrial society had influenced the demands of the ethic itself. Nevertheless, these schemes contained the seeds of that 'logic of domination' which were destined to take root in the nineteenth century. As a consequence, the ideal of an educative society has receded further and further into the background so as to seem merely utopian. In its place, we have the educated society, as Daniel Jenkins is pleased to call it, something very different.

2 The extent of schooling

The wave of industrialization in the nineteenth century created an unprecedented situation which called for strong measures. The evidence of the abuses of child labour revealed by factory commissioners, the statistics of deaths from cholera and other diseases, the novels of Dickens – all these helped to arouse the social conscience. Would voluntary effort have succeeded if it had been left to continue alone? Was the condition of the new industrial working classes so utterly debased that they were unable to help themselves? The historians' verdict, we know, is that any rescue operation had to come from above. But can we be sure that this verdict is necessarily correct?

So far as public literacy is concerned there is evidence to suggest that the ability to read was widespread at the beginning of the nineteenth century and wellnigh universal by 1870.* For the late

*Cf. E. G. West, *Education and the State* (Institute of Economic Affairs, 1970).

eighteenth- and early nineteenth-century philanthropists, however, organized schooling was the obvious solution to the problems posed by industrial urbanization. Hindsight shows their philanthropy to have been a curious blend of altruism and self-interest, of pity and condescension, of piety and the profit motive. If this seems unfair in view of their valiant efforts at a time when most of their contemporaries were standing idly by, critical examination of one account of how a philanthropic act begins may bear it out. Here is Robert Raikes' description of his initiation of the Sunday School movement in Gloucester:

The beginning of this scheme was entirely owing to accident. Some business leading me one morning into the suburbs of the city, where the lowest of the people (who are principally employed in the pin manufactory) chiefly reside, I was struck with concern at seeing a group of children, wretchedly ragged, at play in the streets. I asked an inhabitant whether those children belonged to that part of the town, and lamented their misery and idleness. 'Ah! sir,' said the woman to whom I was speaking, 'could you take a view of this part of the town on a Sunday, you would be shocked indeed; for then the street is filled with multitudes of these wretches, who, released that day from employment, spend their time in noise and riot, playing at "chuck", and cursing and swearing in a manner so horrid as to convey to any serious mind an idea of hell rather than any other place. We have a worthy clergyman [she said] curate of our parish, who has put some of them to school; but upon the Sabbath they are all given up to follow their own inclinations without restraint, as their parents, totally abandoned themselves, have no idea of instilling into the minds of their children principles to which they themselves are entire strangers!'

This conversation suggested to me that it would be at least a harmless attempt, if it were productive of no good, should some little plan be formed to check the deplorable profanation of the Sabbath. I then enquired of the woman, if there were any decent well-disposed women in the neighbourhood who kept schools for teaching to read. I presently was directed to four: to these I applied, and made an agreement with to receive as many children as I should send upon the Sunday, whom they were to instruct in reading and in the Church Catechism. For this I engaged to pay them each a shilling for their day's employment[2].

Hard to say which motive weighed most heavily in Raikes's mind. Could it have been the thought that 4s. was a small price to pay for getting rid of sights and sounds so offensive to genteel folk like himself? If not, why was he not concerned about the social destitution of these ragamuffins during the rest of the week when they were hidden away in the pin factory? The *tone* of the letter speaks for itself. To its credit, however, the Sunday School movement was as open-minded as it was well-meaning (as Raikes said, 'it would be at least a harmless attempt'). If it was shocked by the spectacle of children who felt free 'to follow their own inclinations without restraint', its aims in intervening remained limited. It was never a disciple of the theory that *l'éducation peut tout*.

The same can be said of the monitorial school movement, at any rate in its early stages. 'All who will may send their children to have them educated freely. (The expenses of writing-books excepted.) And those to whom the above offer may not prove acceptable may pay for them at a very modest price.' So read the notice outside Joseph Lancaster's Borough Road School, South-wark, when it opened its doors in 1798. As invitations go, it could hardly have been more courteous. No hint of condescension here.

To its admirers, the success of the monitorial system in reducing an unruly rabble to an orderly, purposeful working group seemed providential, almost miraculous; and to hardheaded business men its cost effectiveness – all this for 3d. per head per week – had a strong appeal. Moreover, its stated objectives – 'to instruct youth in useful learning, in the leading and uncontroverted principles of Christianity, and to train them in the practice of moral habits, conducive to their future welfare, as virtuous men and useful members of society' – reassured those who feared that education might cause the lower orders to rise above their proper station. Lancaster boasted, rightly, that his school was modelled on the factory. It was, indeed, a human conveyer belt on which batches of children were kept constantly on the move. Under such a system, as Robert Owen was not alone in observing, the moral habits which children could not fail to acquire were the ones which Protestantism had always stressed *and* the ones needed in any efficient industrial organization.

The spectrum of British opinion on education during the closing years of the eighteenth century and the early decades of the nineteenth has been faithfully discussed by Harold Silver in *The Concept of Popular Education*:

> The rationalist position is concerned, then, with the concept of justice, because it is unjust for society to deprive the individual of his equal right to the fullest development. It is concerned with the concept of truth, because it is only by diffusing an awareness of the true nature of society and man that the unjust structure of society can be rectified. It is concerned with happiness, because happiness lies not in fettering the individual to his status in an artificially organized society, but precisely in releasing from such fetters and enabling him to participate on a footing of equality in areas of human experience which have been withheld from him. . . . It is a view, finally, which concerns itself with the relationship between the good society and the good man, and with the remoulding of society in order to secure the development of the perfectible qualities of man[3].

Although the hardening of belief in the power of institutions to shape men's lives for the better was only one of many cross-currents of nineteenth-century opinion, it proved to be one of the most influential. As Coleridge saw it, the monitorial system was destined to become 'a vast moral steam-engine'. To the shrewd eyes of captains of industry it opened up managerial possibilities undreamed of by its inventors. All that was needed to make its mechanized practice even more effective was an adequate theory of social engineering – and Owen was sufficiently opinionated to supply just this: 'Any general character, from the worst to the best, from the most ignorant to the most enlightened, may be given to any community, even to the world at large, by the application of the proper means; which means are to a great extent at the command and under the control of those who have influence in the affairs of man.'

There were, of course, many who disagreed violently with Owen and his followers just as there are many nowadays who take exception to Skinner and his. No matter: their opposition to state control was of little or no avail. By mid century it was becoming less and less easy for the voluntary agencies to live up to their claims that they were coping with the ever-growing demand for more schools. Charitable bequests and public subscriptions were no longer capable of meeting the costs of building, staffing and maintenance. For a nation whose existence depended on mass production it seemed that nothing less than mass-production methods of education would serve. The need for universal literacy was the excuse for state intervention. But, as Owen himself admitted, 'the habits of obedience, order, regularity, industry and constant attention [which children "must" learn] . . . are to them *of more importance than merely learning to read, write and account.'*

From Lancaster's 'all who may' to Owen's 'all must' was, therefore, the shortest of steps. The learner's desire, so precious to Rousseau and Godwin, was subordinated to the state's demand. The compulsory principle justified itself, oddly enough in the name of democracy, on the grounds that it was not in the public interest for ordinary parents to make major decisions concerning the upbringing of their children. It was accompanied by an inflated and specious theory of education which, in restricting them to the levels of the Revised Code, showed itself equally scornful of the abilities of ordinary children. By degrees, then, the education system has been erected as a vast public monument, dedicated to the belief that people are clay in the hands of 'those who have influence in the affairs of men'. The latter have always seen to it that their own schools – in the private sector – remain inviolate.

Although parental rights were recognized in the 1870 Act they have been progressively whittled away by subsequent legislation which has placed its emphasis firmly on parental *duties*. In England the election of local school board representatives lasted only a few years: today, the elector has virtually no say in the composition of an Education Committee, and none whatever in their deliberations.

The outcome is a situation in which people are so conditioned to having decisions taken over their heads that they are resigned to the belief that there is nothing they can do about it. Public opinion, pressure groups, protest marches, lobbying MPs, letters to the press, all seem to get nowhere when they seek a confrontation with the hierarchs of the power structure. In Stuart Maclure's judgement, 'Most of the twentieth-century documents have to be read against a background of the growth of power in policy-making and administration at the centre. This growing central power and authority has been the consequence of the growth of government in general, as well of education in particular'[4]. That is the way it is, and that is the way it always has been, we tell ourselves. What is more, the record shows that that is the way it was meant to be from the start. '*Divide and Govern* is as correct a motto for a school as for a cabinet,' as Sir Thomas Bernard remarked as far back as 1812. From the moment when popular schooling became a feasible political policy, it was predictable that the educated ruling class would resort to strategies of domination.

3 The structure of schools

From Monastic Cell to Department Store

Today, more than ever, schools are provided *for* the people. The expansion of the educational services has been accompanied by a growth in economies of scale which has paved the way for administrative gigantism. Time was when it was as easy to build a school as it was to build one's own house. To attempt to do so nowadays seems as futile as to undertake to design and construct one's own jet aircraft. Like other large-scale organizations, the school complex has become so costly and so specialized that it is almost as unthinkable for a group of amateurs to dare to set one up on their own account as it is to imagine that they are free to start printing their own bank-notes. In law, of course, there is nothing to prevent them from making the attempt any more than there is to prevent them from trying out recipes for homemade soap if they wish; but quite apart from the problem of raising the necessary capital, there are so many regulations to fulfil that only cranks, multimillionaires and dedicated idealists would persist against the odds. Everyone else is firmly convinced that schooling is best left in the hands of the authorities just as soapmaking is best left in the hands of big business. The costing of schools, their sites, size, design, contracting, furnishing, staffing, are all decided for us. On the official opening day we are presented with a *fait accompli* and we accept it, usually without demur, because it never occurs to us that we might be consulted.

In tracing the evolution of school-building in Britain it is possible to discern four well-defined stages of development, which may be characterized as follows:

(1) *Medieval*
Originally, the school is housed in or near the church and forms part of it. Its prototype is the monastic cell.

(2) *Renaissance-Reformation*
During the second stage the school is physically separated from the church, but remains small and very simple in its internal organization. Its prototype is the sixteenth- and seventeenth-century grammar school.

(3) *Industrial revolution*
In the third stage two distinct types of school emerge, one modelled on the factory, the other on the stately home. Its prototypes are the nineteenth-century monitorial and elementary schools and the Victorian public school. In both cases there is a notable increase in size, greater differentiation by social class, growing intricacy in internal organization, widening of the curriculum, more elaborate equipment and closer supervision of pupils. Industrial society tends to become school-centred, polarized around these two subsystems, both of which tend to be dissociated from any effective local community controls.

(4) *Late twentieth century*
In the contemporary situation the school takes on the appearance of a huge office block or department store. Its prototype is the comprehensive secondary school. Social differentiation is somewhat less marked and the school complex shows signs of becoming more outward-looking and neighbourhood-centred, with adults as well as children sharing its amenities. Among pupils there is growing resistance to traditional methods of keeping discipline and among parents growing dissatisfaction with bureaucratic regulations. Internally, the building is divided into specialist subject departments and classrooms and has its own library, laboratories, gymnasium, canteen, workshop, theatre, cinema, minimuseum, playing fields, medical inspection centre, plus an

inventory of audio-visual aids which can only be described as lavish. The attempt to convert the school into a resources-for-learning centre is still gathering momentum, but at the same time there is greater willingness to utilize resources which are located outside its walls. As with time-sharing in the use of computers, the escalating costs of equipment are now so prohibitive that it is administratively difficult and educationally undesirable for the school to be organized as if it were self-contained. Officially, all this is recognized, and to some extent allowed for, in the adoption of open plan architectural designs; unofficially, in breakaway ('back to the barn') movements of which the Scotland Road Community Trust, Liverpool, is the first and certainly not the last. The emergence of a fifth stage of development provides the main theme for subsequent chapters.

In 1870 it was still possible, as it had been in 1570, to build and equip a village school accommodating 100 pupils for less than £1,000. By 1971 the net cost *place* limit for primary schools had risen to £257. Today, the starting price for a new comprehensive school may be anything from £500,000 upwards. This phenomenal increase in costs is part of the context in which the recent wholesale expansion of the educational services has taken place. Seeing that rising costs affect housing, jobs, transport, entertainment and other public utilities, it is not surprising that they have also affected the provision and maintenance of schools. Throughout its course, after all, the history of education has run parallel to the history of towns and cities: what more natural, therefore, than to regard the development of schooling as part of the process variously referred to as urbanization, industrialization and modernization? Like it or not, growing up in a sprawling conurbation, if not in a megalopolis, is the common experience of a great many children nowadays. Hence the argument in favour of the school complex as a microcosm of a multifarious society.

It is this characteristic, heterogeneity, and the mutual dependence and interdependence of the several populations comprising an urban centre, which are most germane to the educator. They point to the existence of an urban culture and to the peculiarity and the educational importance of the experience of living in it. An urban location is not merely a given large number of inhabitants, grouped in and around a city centre and spilling over from its traditional physical or administrative boundaries. An urban centre, and by extension an urbanized society, is characterized by a special life-style and a set of relationships in which a large number of identifiable and differentiated social groups are involved. The economy is organized around a complex division of labour and the labour force incorporates a wide differentiation of economic roles and skills. People are joined together into a community more by physical proximity, spatial interaction and mutual dependence, than by sameness of tasks, commonality of past experience, or family relationships. While the administrative boundaries may or may not coincide with the settlement pattern, the urban population is in many respects a separate unit of municipal government. It is further characterized not only by high density of population (and therefore of housing and employment facilities), but also by its wealth of recreational, educational, and general social facilities (such as health and government). Finally, complex transportation systems and extensive use of communications media, whose headquarters are situated in the urban centre, bind the inhabitants together in a network of mass communications[5].

But if urban culture is here to stay it carries with it the threat of cultural shock. The concentration of population and resources which creates the exciting *embarras de richesse* of life in the city can also turn its centre into a ferro-concrete wasteland in which life as it is normally lived is next to impossible. Despite their attractions at holiday times, Manhattan and the City of London may well be considered bad places for kids. If the quality of life remains as indefinable as the scent of a rose, some understanding of its ecology is a prerequisite for educational and town planning alike.

It is no part of the argument to suggest that there is an optimum size for cities or for schools. If there *is* an optimum size it has yet to be found. What has happened in south-east England and along the eastern seaboard of the United States is proof enough that the city can no longer be walled in, and sooner or later it will be seen that the same is true of the school. The difference between the ancient and modern concepts of the school as an institution is the difference between a wren of city like Ely and a brontosaurus like

Tokyo. If the one is outdated because it is too small, the other seems doomed to become extinct because it is too unwieldy. The point, which hardly needs underlining, is that size does affect the ways in which an organization is run. The bigger it grows, the more bureaucratic it becomes and the less amenable to popular control.

Is it in the public interest that schools should be treated in much the same way as other public utilities? Because it is no longer possible for town dwellers to provide their own schools any more than to fetch water from a village pump or to chop firewood to warm their houses does it follow that the educational services must be regarded in the same light as reservoirs and power stations?

The English dislike of large schools springs from a sound instinct. The assumption, if it can be called that, seems to be that institutional size should increase in proportion to the age of the learner. For the very young, the inclination is to opt for nursery classes rather than for nursery schools; for 18-year-olds the prevailing view is that the big polytechnic, or even the multiversity, is the answer. In between there are schools of all shapes and sizes. On the whole, primary schools remain relatively small. So far as the secondary schools are concerned, the problem of 'bigness and bedamnedness' has only arisen in recent years. It is only one aspect, though possibly the most vital one, of the problem which bedevils the education system as a whole.

Post-war developments in education throughout the Western world, and nowhere more acutely than in England, have been largely concerned with the stresses and strains arising from the demand for 'secondary education for all' and the attempt to accommodate widely differentiated social groups within the framework of a school organization whose ethos remains essentially academic and bourgeois. How does one convert a slogan which everyone supports in the name of social justice into an educationally acceptable working formula? In England, the attempt to find such a formula has been hampered by the anti-pathies between the two old-established sub-systems – grammar and elementary – the all too familiar problem of 11-plus. Despite this, the lines of force in British policy-making are slowly converging, as they are in other European countries, on what for want of a better term is called the 'comprehensive principle'. Although there is strong opposition to an all-embracing, allover pattern of secondary schooling, its imposition has been made to seem reasonable, even inevitable, by the growth in economies of scale. More to the point, it has been made possible through the combined operations of a powerful political and bureaucratic directorate which now controls most, if not all, of the resources of manpower and finance. This directorate, moreover, is underpinned by a new and no less powerful managerial class who occupy the key positions in the schools and colleges. While taking good care to placate public opinion by seeming to go through the motions of joint consultation, it can afford to ignore the representations of the numerous voluntary associations and pressure groups which have sprung up in recent years, and from which it meets increasingly stiff resistance. The directorate's is a world of Royal Commissions, of Boards, of committees and officialdom.

In singling out the comprehensive school as the prototype of late twentieth-century organizational development it is not intended to convey the impression that its adoption will necessarily become general. Despite the differences between the Labour and Conservative party lines, it certainly looks as though the comprehensive school represents the shape of things to come. If so, further developments along the lines which have given us the multistorey tenement block and the supercolossal oil tanker must be anticipated.

The prospect seems a good deal less alarming when it is recalled that more than half of our primary schools were built before 1903, and that most secondary modern schools date from the era of the Hadow reorganization. Both *The Education of the Adolescent* (1926) and *The Primary School* (1931) advocated a curriculum conceived in terms of activity and experience, and the building programmes which followed were to some extent designed to allow greater freedom for the exercise of the 'practical intelligence' as the Hadow Report was pleased to call it. For the sake of removing the bad image from which the elementary school had suffered since its inception, and in the interests of 'parity of esteem', the new secondary modern schools were given special treatment as well as every inducement to find and follow a way of life of their own. Some succeeded in doing so, but in nine cases out of ten the daily and weekly routine of chalk and talk continued as before. The bright glass boxes in which they were housed did little to alleviate their sense of inferiority, even if at times they aroused the envy of the grammar schools.

In passing, it is tempting to remark that the 1926 decision to make a 'clean break' at 11-plus and to replace the old vertical division between elementary and grammar sub-systems with a horizontal one between primary and secondary stages owed more to the arrival on the scene of the motor-car and the school bus than it did to educational ideas or even administrative convenience. In the USA, where a similar reorganization (consolidation) of the countless thousands of small school districts was proceeding apace at the same time, rapid improvements in road transportation produced effects more traumatic than their impact on the all-age school in England and Wales. The position of the Little Red Schoolhouse, so dear to Americans as the symbol of the grassroots tradition, was secure only so long as children had to walk to school. More so than any other single factor, it was the combustion engine which first weakened local community control and reinforced the argument in favour of larger administrative units.

With the departure of their senior pupils, and with the pressure of the all-important 11-plus examination gradually easing, the infants and junior schools were left tolerably free to follow their own devices. As 'feeders' for the secondary school, they remained for the most part relatively small establishments. Such structural changes as they underwent were negligible compared with the massive ones which have led to the comprehensive Gargantua. Most of those built between 1870 and 1918 had a central hall with classrooms leading off from it. During the inter-war period a veranda-type plan with classrooms arranged in rows round an open-air quadrangle was favoured. This provided an environment which was at least light and airy, but the classroom remained the basic unit, and teachers who wished to try out group methods or engage in practical projects frequently complained that conditions of work were little better than they had been under the conventional set-up.

It is often said, and with some justice, that the most worthwhile innovations in British education since the end of World War II have stemmed from the much-abused efforts of a minority of primary school teachers to translate child-centred theory into everyday practice. How far this liking for 'progressive' methods – group work, projects, drama, music-making, use of apparatus, integrated day, team teaching etc. – has been responsible for the growing interest in open plan designs and how far such methods have been stimulated by the latest primary school buildings themselves is one of those chicken-or-egg questions which need not detain us. First Hertfordshire, then one by one other county LEAs, earned a reputation for schools whose proportions and décor were aesthetically pleasing and whose layout offered their occupants opportunities for spacious living.

Open plan, like team teaching, is an elastic term. At its most elaborate, it tends to be associated with the doctrinaire jargon of ministry-sponsored building bulletins: at its simplest, it means knocking down partition walls to create work and play areas in which teachers and children from more than one classroom can spread themselves. In a sense, it signalizes a return to the original schoolhouse in which pupils were not graded by age, ability or attainment. To that extent, it may be seen as the first step in the direction of a free school.

In terms of group dynamics, the effect of opening up the interior of the building can be heartening: teachers learn the advantages of co-operating with each other, auxiliary staff and parents get more of a look-in, and the children find it a welcome release from the normal deskbound learning situation.

Long confinement to the classroom, unfortunately, has fostered a me-and-my-children attitude which might almost be called the hallmark of the teaching profession. Co-operation sounds fine in principle, but British individualism likes its privacy, and to many teachers the idea of having to work alongside colleagues, let alone para-professionals and parents, seems peculiarly distasteful. Without a blackboard behind them and a captive audience in front, they feel insecure. They are not prepared for theatre in the round. Supervising the activities of pupils who are scattered around all over the place can be as exasperating as trying to keep track of a pack of hounds turned loose in a rabbit warren. The eggbox building, moreover, has left an all but indelible impression on our ideas about the ways in which an efficiently organized school ought to be run. Enlightened HMIs may look kindly on the family atmosphere and informality induced by open plan arrangements, and register their approval of what, to them, looks like a hive of industry. To others, the new order savours too much of disorder. Teachers are not alone in having preconceived notions about their jobs: parents and pupils, too, often say quite frankly that they would prefer to have a 'proper school'.

Some visitors to schools of this type . . . allege that conditions become chaotic and the children's work too disconnected, with the result that grounding in the 'basic subjects' (usually defined very narrowly) is neglected. And where the children appear to be working happily and purposefully, it is often said that the better schools of this kind attract particularly talented staff and that the average teacher could not do it. Nobody who has seen a well-designed and properly organized school of this type in operation can doubt that considerable teaching skills are required. But what seems to be needed are not so much those indefinable qualities associated with brilliant individual performances as a grasp of essential principles and a capacity to play one's part in a complex teaching situation, for which specific training can be given. Auxiliary staff can also make a real contribution and may be regarded in the same light as the paramedical staff who support the work of the modern doctor[6].

Not all the criticism of open plan schooling can be discounted as emanating from hostile witnesses, but a great deal of it can. Ironically although anything faintly 'progressive' in education invariably gets a bad press in this country, foreign visitors sing its praises. The impartial verdict must be that the conventional primary school is simply not good enough. It may well be, as Susan Isaacs acknowledged, that 'really to let the child learn by doing would involve an immense advance in all the material setting of school life, as well as in the number of staff and variety of equipment', and that 'there is little to be done with large classes of children, ranging in ability from the nearly defective to the very superior, but to keep them quiet and talk to them', and it may be that the well-publicized achievements of a handful of schools in a few semi-rural counties are merely the exceptions which prove the rule[7]. Even so, they shine like good deeds in the naughty world of the statutory system. Among others, their salient features include: (a) less emphasis on formal instruction, (b) a heuristic approach to learning, (c) closer involvement of parents, aides and other interested outsiders, (d) greater attention to individual differences, (e) mingling of different age and ability groups, (f) a less inhibited reliance on the pupils' initiative and motivation,

(g) a refusal to admit any hard and fast distinction between curricular and extracurricular activities, (h) easier, friendlier relationships between children and adults.

It is arguable that hardly any of these features can be reproduced in a large school catering for older children. A family atmosphere may be admirably cosy in the infants' room, but is it appropriate for sixth formers or for recalcitrant school-leavers? On the whole, secondary schools are much bigger than primary schools, more constrained by external examination requirements, and accordingly more hierarchical in their organization.

The curious thing about this kind of argument is that it flies in the face of developmental psychology. Teenagers, surely, are the very ones who stand to benefit most from being treated as if they were responsible agents. Other things being equal, the inference, surely, is that methods which have been shown to work well with younger children will prove to be even more successful with older ones.

At the secondary stage, however, other things are not equal. The primordial link between the grammar school and the university, typified by the relationship between Winchester and New College, Oxford, has been extended and perpetuated in modern times mainly through the public examination system. Today it manifests itself in the annual ritual of the paperchase for O- and A-level awards. The grammar school's pre-eminence is jealously guarded and so carefully preserved as to prejudice all our thinking about the learning process. It was the unassailable prestige of its long-established tradition of academic scholarship which swelled the ranks of sixth formers after 1944, which caused the secondary modern school to ape its betters and settle for a good-for-nothing certificate, and which distorted, when it did not actually frustrate, the genesis of the comprehensive school. If this threefold charge sounds over-rhetorical one has only to consider the facts.

Between 1950 and 1966 the total school population rose by 24 per cent but the numbers staying on in full-time attendance beyond the age of fifteen increased from 290,354 to 782,027. During the same period the number of passes in individual subjects at O-level trebled (427,038 to 1,256,480). At A-level the increase was, if anything, more spectacular (77,435 in 1952 to 254,788 in 1965). The sixth form, long regarded as the keystone of the English system of education, now assumed the overreaching importance of an institution in its own right. The more top-heavy a grammar school grew, the greater its reputation. It led the way to university entrance, and the rest followed – at a distance.

Meanwhile the secondary modern school, all dressed up with nowhere to go, had been left to carry on as best it could with the make-do, make-believe curriculum envisaged for it in *The Education of the Adolescent*. For a decade or so it did its best, only to give up the unequal struggle and tag along behind the grammar school in the O-level handicap stakes. It could hardly be blamed for feeling drawn in two directions. At the upper end of its ability range was a sizeable proportion of pupils who had failed the 11-plus examination by the narrowest and most dubious of margins and who would have been allocated to a full-length academic course had they been domiciled in Scotland: what more natural, therefore, than that their parents and teachers should press for tangible recognition in the shape of a national leaving certificate? While the intention of leaving the secondary school free from any sort of external examination requirements was educationally sound, it was socially unrealistic. Courses built round 'projects' and 'centres of interest' failed to satisfy the hunger for certificates. If it seems unduly harsh to say that it failed, the search for a viable alternative to the one form of secondary education which commanded universal respect was vitiated from the start. The situation might have been more promising if the technical secondary schools had been given the support they deserved: instead, they were quietly cold-shouldered and kept in a state of arrested development. With the clamour for paper qualifications intensifying year by year some compromise had to be found and, in a weak moment, the Beloe Committee took the line of least resistance by offering a consolation prize, the Certificate of Secondary Education.

To its credit, the Newsom Report was suitably sceptical about the wisdom of this latest step:

> We are convinced that for a substantial number of pupils public examinations would be entirely inappropriate, and for a considerable number of others they would be appropriate over only a small part of their school work. In other words, we do not think that external examinations will provide a valid major incentive for many of the pupils with whom we are concerned. A longer school life will need to justify itself in other terms. . . .

We likewise strongly endorse the warning that the tendency of examinations to limit freedom in the curriculum and to restrict experiment could be especially harmful to pupils in the lower ability ranges, at a time when freedom to experiment with new educational patterns is most needed. We would reiterate the statement of the Crowther Report:

> In some subjects a good modern school education seems to us very difficult to reconcile with an external examination. If it is right, and we believe it is, that the approach to knowledge should be as little abstract as possible for boys and girls of ordinary ability if full use is to be made of their environment, then a good deal of the approach to history and the social sciences, to geography and to biology will be dictated by the character of the place in which the school is. In practical subjects also, the right teaching approach does not lie through a series of graded exercises standing by themselves, which is what a large-scale examination tends to encourage, however much the examiners may wish to discourage it.

> Since, however, examinations are here to stay, and as time goes on the tendency is always for more rather than fewer pupils to be involved, we must seek means to minimize the more adverse effects[8].

Again, it was the overriding importance attached to sixth form scholarship which dominated the initial planning of the all-through comprehensive school.

> The LCC decided upon a size of up to 2,000 places for its schools for two reasons. Firstly, there is difficulty in providing adequately for sixth form work if the total intake of a comprehensive school is too small. Secondly, the provision of sites was a severe problem. It was felt that the minimum-sized entry for the academic fraction of a comprehensive school should not be smaller than the units which had in the past been found to be efficient in the grammar schools. It was suggested that 'In practice a one-stream entry (total 160 pupils) is found to be too small and even a two-stream entry (about 330 pupils in all) does not provide effective alternative courses. The three-streamed school (480) works very well, but a four-stream school is usually even more efficient[9].

In other words, the interests of the broad mass of pupils (supposedly the *raison d'être* of comprehensive schools) were sacrificed for the sake of 'the academic fraction', and the 'units which had in the past been found to be efficient in the grammar schools' were the measuring rods used in making plans for the future. They still are. In his essay on 'The essential conditions for the success of a comprehensive school', Dr Rhodes Boyson reaffirms the conviction that:

> An upper and lower academic sixth of 45 boys each requires a school with an entry of 360 boys each year if one accepts the present figure that one-eighth of an age group can take two or more A-levels. This will mean a school of 2,000. If one expects the percentage of boys capable of two A-level courses to rise to 20 per cent in the next few years and settle at this figure then a school of 1,400 with a fully balanced ability intake would bring an academic sixth form of sufficient size. Such a school can be smaller in a favoured town like a south coast resort or would need to be larger in a town with bad housing and a history of deprivation. To attempt to meet the fear which people have of the size required for all-through comprehensive schools by cutting them to schools of below 1,000 is to court eventual failure or uneconomic sixth form classes whilst to break such schools up by horizontal divisions and transfers at 13, 14 and 16 is to destroy the unity of secondary school learning and bring another decline in educational standards. Good comprehensive schools generally mean large comprehensive schools and they can only be reduced in size at great risk[10].

This is a fair specimen of patrician thinking, typical of the Black Paper mentality. It takes A-level scholarship as the sole touchstone of 'success' and fixes its 'standards' to suit those of the academic community. It is all the more pernicious for its deference to a 'tradition' which the historical record shows to have been largely fictitious. This is how the logic of domination casts its spells, forever bidding the unwary to fetish-worship.

While it may be hoped that English empiricism and English fair play will be proof against the subterfuges of the hard-liners and the *arrière-garde*, the auguries are not favourable. The trend towards ever larger administrative units shows no signs of being reversed, and, no allover pattern having yet been imposed, secondary schooling in this country looks like being something of a mixed grill in the foreseeable future. So long as official, professional and public opinion about the nature and purpose of secondary schooling remains as one-track as it is, the feasibility of any common curriculum is bound to be called in question.

The school complex, as represented by the all-through, all-purpose comprehensive school, marks the culmination of an organizational development which began in the austerity of the monastic cell. Or is it the *reductio ad absurdum*? So far the objection to the secondary school as a kind of mini-polytechnic has been on the grounds that its elaboration rules out the possibility of local community control. The point at issue is in fact more subtle. It may help to elucidate it if we compare the administrative set-up of a 'closed' institution – the university being as good an example as any – with that of an open (free) school.

In the first place, a university is a regional centre of higher learning, not a local one. Secondly, it serves an academic community which has always kept itself apart from the rest of society and operated as a 'closed shop'. Hence no one feels upset on learning that the University of X has decided to purchase a cyclotron, to install a closed-circuit television network, or to found half a dozen new chairs. The thought that Midas himself could not muster the wealth needed for a twentieth-century *cité universitaire* is not all that troublesome. Student protesters may disagree, but the public sees no reason why the university court and senate should not conduct their business behind closed doors. It is generally conceded that academic freedom needs to be safeguarded. Being largely independent, the university lays down its own regulations; anyone who fails or refuses to comply with them has only himself to blame if he is excluded.

The various ways in which an open or a free school might operate will be discussed in subsequent chapters: enough for the moment to say that it could not, like the university, operate in isolation from the community. Parental opinion, local wishes and views, would all affect the decisions taken there. As things are, however, the typical secondary school is to all intents and purposes a closed institution. The man in the street who ventures inside feels like an intruder. He does not *belong* there and any suggestion that it belongs to him is too utterly remote to be entertainable. As he threads his way through its labyrinth of buildings – science block, workshop, catering department, art and craft studios, assembly hall, teaching wings and the rest – he cannot help feeling overawed. This House of Intellect, it seems, has many mansions. The machinery in the workshop block would not look out of place in the most up-to-date industrial plant, and the model flats in the domestic science wing would be the envy of many a hotelier. Finding out who does what in this mighty maze can be as mystifying for the chance visitor as finding his way around it. Headmaster, deputy headmaster, secretary, senior housemaster, director of studies, heads of houses, heads of subjects – to which of these should he address his inquiries, he wonders nervously? All very impressive, but somehow (just why he cannot explain) it leaves him cold.

> Classrooms may be varied to include laboratory, workshop, gymnasium and year abroad, but this is all scholastic space – sanitized, sealed off from the unclean world, made fit for children and for the transmission of knowledge. In this specialized environment, knowledge must be transmitted, it cannot merely be encountered, since in most cases it has been taken out of its natural habitat[11].

Reimer's distinction between the 'natural habitat' and the 'specialized environment' of learning is essentially the same as the one drawn by Dewey between 'life situations' and the 'divorce of school from life'. It is a plea for a theory and practice of education more personal, experiential than the cognitive, conceptual one usually propounded by pedagogues.

That the all-purpose secondary school is a 'specialized environment' is obvious enough, but if it is indeed 'divorced from life', how, if at all, can it be returned to a 'natural habitat' of learning? In *The Adolescent Society*, Coleman concludes that:

> In a rapidly changing, highly rationalized society, the 'natural processes' of education in the family are no longer adequate. They have been replaced by a more formalized institution that is set apart from the rest of society. . . . In sum, then, the general point is: our adolescents today are cut off, probably more than ever before, from the adult society. They are still oriented toward fulfilling their parents' desires, but they look very much to their peers for approval as well. Consequently our society has

within its midst a set of small teenage societies, which focus teenage interest and attitudes on things far removed from adult responsibilities, and which may develop standards that lead away from those goals established by the larger society. . . . As has been evident throughout this research, the variation among the schools in the status of scholastic achievement is not nearly so striking as the fact that in all of them, academic achievement did not 'count' for as much as other activities in the school. . . . The relative unimportance of academic achievement . . . suggests that the adolescent subcultures in these schools exert a rather strong deterrent to academic achievement[12].

All of which reinforces the argument advanced earlier, to wit, that if young children stand to gain a great deal from self-initiated, peer-group activities, teenagers stand to gain more. As they experience it, school-bound learning *is* artificial in the way that a simulation exercise differs from the actual performance of a task on-the-job. The school complex serves as a working model of society – model flats for the girls, model workbenches for the boys – and provides for a wide range of simulation exercises, many of them absorbing, some of them quite invaluable. The model is highly elaborate and needs experts to keep it in running order, not to mention a plentiful supply of spare parts and a steadily increasing flow of cash. But no matter how assiduously it is maintained and expanded, the model cannot reproduce all the resources which a modern society has at its disposal. The school's attempt to put all its eggs in one basket is misconceived. The days of its enclosure are numbered. Very soon there will be no point in its trying, and less in pretending, to believe that learning can be 'cabin'd, cribb'd, confin'd' in this way.

We could do with simpler, homelier models.

References

1. J. Bowen, *A History of Western Education*, vol. I (Methuen, 1972).
2. D. W. Sylvester, *Educational Documents 1800–1816* (Methuen, 1970), pp. 254–5.
3. H. Silver, *The Concept of Popular Education* (MacGibbon & Kee, 1965), p. 56.
4. J. Stuart Maclure, *Educational Documents, England and Wales 1816–1968* 2nd ed. (Chapman & Hall, 1965).

5. Max Eckstein, 'Toward a strategy of urban educational study' in *The Year Book of Education 1970 – Education in Cities* (Evans, 1970), p. 20.
6. M. Seaborne, *Primary School Design* (RKP, 1971), p. 70.
7. Cf. H. Entwistle, *Child-centred Education* (Methuen, 1970), p. 194.
8. Report of the Advisory Council on Education, *Half Our Future* (HMSO, 1963), paragraphs 244–6.
9. R. Cole, *Comprehensive Schools in Action* (Oldbourne, 1964), p. 84.
10. Rhodes Boyson, 'The essential conditions for the success of a comprehensive school' in C. B. Cox and A. E. Dyson (eds.) *The Black Papers on Education* (Davis-Poynter, 1971), p. 158.
11. Everett Reimer, *School is Dead* (Penguin Books, 1971), p. 39.
12. J. S. Coleman, *The Adolescent Society* (Free Press, Glencoe, 1961), pp. 4, 9, 265.

Section IV

DESCHOOLING IN ACTION

DESCHOOLING IN ACTION

In practice, deschooling has already begun in many places, not necessarily under that name, of course, and not necessarily in extreme forms. In theory, deschooling now enjoys a wide measure of approval in quarters where it might be least expected, notably among the ranks of some of our leading educationists.

Professor Ben Morris, for one, is left wondering whether it is possible that we are on the wrong track altogether. Does increasing the school-leaving age make sense, he asks? Are educational institutions really offering the kind of nourishment that youth needs? Are we really offering something that will raise the level of skill in the country? Are the aims of a highly educated and a highly skilled population incompatible, and can we afford it for everyone on the planet, or only for an élite? Broadly speaking, his answers agree closely with the arguments pursued in previous chapters, and to that extent may serve as a summary:

It is a fact that there is a fairly widespread disenchantment among young people with the educational system and, more generally, with adult values. I am not talking about a small number of disaffected, disturbed adolescents, though there are those, but about a more general attitude which can be understood in the context of growing up today, the mismatch

E

of professions/practices of institutions and the speed of change.

While it is a biological fact that adolescence and puberty occur earlier, society delays school-leaving and with it the time when the young can play an adult role in society: they live in a social limbo. Meanwhile over the last quarter century the rise in divorce rates and women at work has meant a weakening of family ties: the family is neither such a secure, nor such a suffocating structure. And a first generation of higher-educated youth – which the present expansion in universities and polytechnics has created – always produces problems. All these pressures add up to an earlier search for personal identity and a disinclination to delay satisfaction. . . .

The common theory of education attributes four functions: instructional, socialization, custodial and classificatory (i.e. collecting and labelling people for their later roles). These functions don't add up to an education, or to a means of helping young people to grow up into an adult world. But is this picture correct, and how far are we trying to separate the instructional and guidance aspects of education?

It is not surprising that there is such disenchantment of the young for the old. In the US and our own country there is already a counter-culture, and it is encouraging to note that this movement includes with the dropouts the young radicals who aim to modify the social structure that they reject. . . . Personally, I would like to see some of the old aims of education realized, which would lead to a new culture. There is no doubt that education is a most revolutionary weapon, a (potentially) major force for change. I believe that education must embody something of a zest for life, frankly, a joy. We could look with profit at some of our new primary schools where the children enjoy learning. This in itself is rather a great revolution. Secondly, I want people to develop their powers of reason and imagination. Too often education gives knowledge out of context. With such ventures as the new mathematics we are seeing the spirit of inquiry being embodied into the curricula, and this contributes to the whole process by which people enjoy learning. Education must also develop tolerance and enlargement of human sympathies. This is probably the most pressing need of all. . . . Education should develop responsibility. And people can't exercise responsibility until they are given it – which fact is behind the move towards participation. Lastly, we need to develop the powers of discrimination, of distinguishing between good and bad: not only in morals but in all spheres. Powers of discrimination exist in all children, but they can only be developed through situations with which they are already familiar.

To meet the new institutional requirements of education we must redesign a lifelong system that is permanently available to all at any age, and in time reduce the school-leaving age rather than raising it. There must be more flexibility between courses and institutions. There must be greater use of the media and resources for learning, but these things must remain subordinate to the teacher: technology makes a good servant but a bad master. And the relationship between teacher and taught must change from the dominant/submissive to 'learning through context and discovery'. This is not to say that there should be equality between teacher and pupil, but more of a partnership.

In general, therefore, we have got to envisage changes in the institutional structure which will entail less hierarchy and more community[1].

What, then, do these changes in institutional structure amount to in practice, and where can they be seen taking place? It is true that none of the eight examples which follow lives up to the idea of a free school in every respect, yet each in its modest way illustrates a dimension of freedom which has either been denied or lost sight of during the past century. Among these are: (1) freedom of access – the right of parents, teachers and children to work and play together on a partnership basis, to share the same facilities and participate in matters of common interest, (2) freedom to learn in one's own time, in one's own way – i.e. without being required to attend a particular place during fixed hours and for a fixed period, (3) freedom to establish, organize and manage schools other than those provided by the education authorities, (4) freedom to exploit resources for learning which are located in the community at large.

Granted, these are not the only desiderata and the free school of the future may envisage dimensions of freedom a good deal wider than these, but they are enough to be going on with, at any rate in a situation in which all of us need to learn to walk before we can presume to run. In the USA 'The adoption of the mini-school as a possible antidote has been rapid. But the rhetoric – too often – has run far ahead of performance.'[2] Most of the way-out free schools have a pitiably short half-life, warns Kozol[3]. *Pace* Illich, deschooling does not necessarily mean the total abolition of the existing system: it *does* mean relaxing many of the regulations, requirements and practices which have outlived their original purpose and to which we cling at our peril. At our peril, because if we do not relax them the young will do it for us.

The accounts which follow are necessarily compressed and the examples chosen all too few. No doubt the radical reader would prefer more exciting ones. Freedom of access, he will say, is no longer in serious dispute – and there are in Britain today any number of establishments, secondary as well as primary, which answer to the description of an open school. As for freedom to learn in one's own way, in one's own time, it has been made possible in a wide variety of curriculum projects as well as in the field of educational technology.

Collectively, nevertheless, these eight examples may be taken as representative, or at least indicative, of current trends which are certain to continue in the years ahead. To repeat, what we are now witnessing is the beginning of a movement which will eventually see the end of the secondary school as an institution for the enforced confinement of young people. During the Railway Age a train was a steam-engine with a chimney belching smoke: in an Age of Technology the chimney and the smoke disappear. In the same way, the school as we have come to know it may now be regarded as a proper study for industrial archaeology.

But no amount of doctrinaire theory will convince the doubting Thomases that practical alternatives to schooling already exist. Hence the need for straightforward descriptions of current projects which point towards the realization of the idea of the free school.

References

1. Ben Morris, 'Changes in education', in *The Use of Resources*, Study Conference 71–49 Coombe Lodge Report, IV, 19 (1972).

2. Diane Divoky, 'New York's mini-schools', *New York Saturday Review* (18 December 1971).
3. Jonathan Kozol, 'Free schools: a time for candor', *New York Saturday Review* (4 March 1972).

1 The open school

(a) Countesthorpe College

To say that the ecology of educational innovation is dimly understood is an understatement. In the bad old days of the 11-plus it used to be said that equality of opportunity in England was largely a matter of geographical luck; although this may no longer be quite so obviously true, some local authorities are more go-ahead than others and the general pattern rather resembles a patchwork quilt. Some regional arrangements are evidently more conducive to forward thinking than others. Of all the counties, Leicestershire is perhaps the one which has most frequently been singled out for special mention in recent years as a trendsetter in the planning of new-style primary and secondary schools, and as an authority whose record of fruitful collaboration between administrators, academics and teachers is second to none.

If an account of Scotland Road Free School reads like a hard-luck story, Countesthorpe College may be said to have been born with a silver spoon in its mouth. It occupies a multipurpose campus which has been specially designed to integrate the local secondary school, youth clubs, evening institute, social and recreational organizations into an educational community centre. More important, it also represents an attempt to bring shared decision making down to the lowest possible levels and to make participatory democracy a going concern. Its elaborate constitution, which delegates power and responsibility left, right and centre, owes a great deal to the enlightened and shrewd thinking of its first warden, Tim McMullen, formerly director of the Nuffield Resources-for-Learning Project.

Although the college complex is planned as a single entity, with adults, young people and children sharing the same facilities and frequently working and playing alongside each other, its activities

can best be outlined under the separate headings of (a) the school,
(b) the community educational programme.

(a) *The School*

At present the school accommodates some 600 high school boys
and girls (ages 11–14) and 3–400 upper school students (ages
14–16). By 1975 the high school pupils will have been transferred
to their own building and the upper school will then consist of
1440 mixed students with a large sixth form.

The academic policy and the day-to-day running of the school
is in the hands of a representative body – the 'moot' – whose
legislative and executive powers are virtually absolute, being
subject only to the regulations of the county education authority
and the laws of the land. The warden remains personally responsible for all decisions taken by the moot, but has delegated the
right to make such decisions and has agreed that under no circumstances will he exercise the right of veto – though he *does*
reserve the right to resign if an important decision is taken which
offends his conscience. For the time being, the moot consists of all
members of the professional staff, part-time as well as full-time,
of the school and the community college. Upper school students
are allowed to attend its meetings and to speak, but for the present
not to vote. Ways and means of extending student participation
are to be reviewed in the light of developments as the intake of
16–18-year-olds increases. As things are, an elected school
council with a student majority has the right to determine non-
academic affairs.

In turn, the moot delegates powers to four committees, each
consisting of a quarter of the staff, which meet weekly outside
school hours, and elect their own chairman and secretary. These
prepare agenda papers for the full moot and discuss any matters of
policy or administration which need immediate attention. In
addition, a special subcommittee is responsible for making recom-
mendations for staff appointments, including the shortlisting,
entertaining and interviewing of candidates. (The warden and his
deputies are available if advice is needed, but have let it be known
that they will only attend when appointments are made *if invited.*)

Purpose-built, the school incorporates many of the features of
advanced open plan architectural design including lecture theatres,
conference rooms, wall-to-wall carpeted spaces, lounges, labora-

tories, workshops and other amenities. More to the point, it utilizes a wealth of ideas derived from experimental methodology and curriculum development in this country as well as abroad. Its system of government, with its interlocking two-way relations between warden and staff, staff and pupils, is intended to foster active co-operation and an allround acceptance of personal responsibility.

This involves putting a much greater stress on the children in developing a sense of self-discipline than on obeying an imposed system of rules and regulations. What we say is that the rules of the land, the laws, must be obeyed, as must the regulations of the LEA, that otherwise the guide for conduct is 'social' rather than 'antisocial' behaviour, but not the staff's particular standards of taste, e.g. in what you wear or how you speak. The method of preventing antisocial behaviour is more by exerting our constant pressure – and increasingly that of public opinion with the school – than by using deterrent punishments.

Countesthorpe differs from the ordinary comprehensive secondary school in other ways. In the first place, mixed ability grouping is the rule and streaming is restricted mainly to the teaching of foreign languages. In the field of the humanities the division of the curriculum into self-contained subjects like English, geography, history and religious instruction, is replaced by contextual areas of study – 'the individual and the group', 'work', 'education', 'law and order', etc. All pupils follow a broad common core course until the age of sixteen so that early specialization is avoided. On the other hand, pupils are given the opportunity to choose from a wide selection of options for up to one quarter of their time. All first and second year pupils who are not taking a foreign language have two free half-days a week to encourage independent study and to help them to plan their own work. In some optional courses, e.g. motor vehicle engineering and physics, the composition of the group is largely determined by self-selection. In mathematics and general science the emphasis in the common course is placed on problem-solving rather than on the learning of facts and techniques. Each pupil is expected to work to the level of his estimated potential, and individual differences are catered for through a judicious pastoral care and guidance organization. No form of awarding marks, orders of merit or prizes is considered appropriate: at the same time it is recognized that pupils and parents need to be kept regularly informed of the progress they are making – and of their apparent chances of academic success in the GCE or CSE examinations at least before the end of the fourth year.

The school sets itself five *classes* of learning objectives as follows:

A. *Knowledge* (i.e. understanding of facts, principles and concepts)
  1. The student's knowledge of himself, his relationships with others, both individuals and groups, of groups and their behaviour, of local, national and international aspects of society.
  2. The student's knowledge of his environment and man's interaction with it.
  3. Knowledge required for the learning of a skill or the practice of a creative or expressive activity.
B. *Logical Processes*
  1. Analysis of a problem – recall of relevant principles and concepts, selection and trial of these and testing of solution.
  2. Analysis of a problem – assembly of all relevant facts, construction and testing of hypotheses.
  3. Analysis of a problem – recognition of relevant criteria, examination of possible hypotheses and justification of one of these.
  4. Recognition of the emotional and rational elements in any argument.
C. *Skills*
  1. Communication skills – oral, social, reading, writing, numerical, symbolic, graphic, foreign languages, etc.
  2. Performance skills – in music, craft, games, etc.
D. *Creative and Expressive Activities*
  1. Ability to participate in arts, crafts, literature, music, movement, drama, applied science, athletics and sports.
  2. Ability to produce original ideas, to think laterally rather than convergently.
E. *Personal Characteristics and Attitudes*
  1. Ability to understand, so far as possible, one's own behaviour and the motives that lie behind it.

2. Ability to understand other people's behaviour and the motives behind it.
3. Tolerance of the differences between one's self and others.
4. Development and recognition of one's personal moral code.
5. Understanding that other moral codes exist and have equal validity for those who hold them.
6. Ability to distinguish between that part of one's own moral code that is based on belief and that part which is based on reason.
7. Understanding the different personal and social relationships that arise from egotistical and altruistic actions.
8. Ability to maintain one's own integrity as an individual within a group.
9. Ability to control one's individual desires for the group purpose.
10. Ability to co-operate with others for a common purpose.
11. Ability to organize one's own work and play.
12. Ability to recognize and strive for distant goals.
13. Ability to recognize the nature of social situations and to find the right reactions to them.

This checklist is worth reproducing *in extenso* if only because it reflects the careful thinking that underlies the organization of Countesthorpe College.

Just as what is learnt is to some degree different, so is how it is learnt [says the Warden]. This involves much work either by oneself or in small groups using material either specially prepared by the staff or by bodies such as the Nuffield Foundation. It also makes use of film, recorded television programmes and uses tape recorders as alternative methods to writing for recording results. . . . On the whole, such work is carried out in groups of mixed ability and attainment, the individuals either progressing at different rates, or doing work at different depths, or following different programmes. Progressively, in some subjects, groups will become homogeneous in the sense that some will opt for work with an examination bias, others not. The periods which the children work are longer than usual, half or whole mornings or afternoons, but with choice and variety of approach within each period.

One final point of interest: several adult classes take place on the premises during school time and pupils are encouraged to join classes and clubs organized by the department of community education in the evening and at weekends. Mixed classes of old and young are envisaged in the future when the school has its full complement of sixth formers.

(b) *The Department of Community Education*
The department is responsible for a varied programme of adult education and youth activities in the college. Its tutors are members of the school staff but have a joint allegiance to school and community. The community council comprises elected representatives from adult classes, youth clubs and affiliated societies, together with six members of the governing body and the warden (or the director of community studies) who acts as secretary. On behalf of the council, a management committee and a programme subcommittee assist the staff tutors in the day-to-day running of the centre. There is a nominal college membership fee (25p) and an affiliation scheme which enables common-interest groups to set up their own clubs and organize their own programmes. In so far as the LEA budget allocation allows, the council is prepared to help such groups by charging minimal rents for the use of rooms and other facilities. Everyone is free to attend meetings of the council, but voting is restricted to elected member representatives. In 1970–1 there were 680 students enrolled in adult classes, 300 in affiliated societies and 160 under the age of eighteen in evening classes. Family groups of parents and children sometimes work together in the same class.

The *Countesthorpe College Community News* keeps people in the locality informed about what is going on and what courses are being offered. Glancing through its pages is like reading the *Radio Times*: the range of choice is impressively wide. A typical weekly schedule, culled at random from issue No. 6 (18 August 1971) includes the following:

1. *Daytime Courses*
Pottery   Tuesdays 9.45–11.45 (21 weeks)
Homecrafts   Tuesdays 9.45–11.45 (21 weeks)
Modern poetry (university course)   Tuesdays 10–11.30 (10 weeks)

Speech therapy clinic	Tuesday mornings
A fresh look at cookery	Mondays 1.30–3.00 (11 weeks)
Homecraft for the retired	Wednesdays 2.00–4.00 (11 weeks)
Dressmaking	Thursdays 9.45–11.45 (21 weeks)
Painting for pleasure	Thursdays 9.45–11.45 (21 weeks)
Return to teaching group	Thursdays 9.45–11.45 (22 weeks)
Nursery play group	Tuesdays and Thursdays 10–12
Ladies' keep fit	Thursdays 1.30–3.00 (22 weeks)
Millinery	Thursdays 1.30–3.00 (21 weeks)
Your child's world at home and school	Thursdays 1.30–3.00 (11 weeks)

2. *Evening Courses*

The amateur's greenhouse	Mondays 7.15–9.15 (5 weeks)
Basketball	Mondays 8.30–10 (21 weeks)
Car maintenance	Mondays 7.30–9.30 (21 weeks)
Cookery – unusual starters and exciting sweets	Mondays 7.00–9 (6 weeks)
Drivers' club	Mondays Monthly at 7.30
French circle	Mondays 7.30–9.30 (21 weeks)
Gardening – trees, shrubs and roses	Mondays 7.15–9.15 (5 weeks)
Golf	Mondays 7.00–8.30 (11 weeks)
Improving your yoga	Mondays 7.15–9.15 (21 weeks)
Local history (WEA course)	Mondays 7.30–9 (11 weeks)
Painting, drawing and printing	Mondays 7.15–9.15 (21 weeks)
Art workshop	Tuesdays 7.15–9.15 (21 weeks)
Be a better driver	Tuesdays 7.30–9.30 (11 weeks)
Beginners' French	Tuesdays 7.30–9.30 (21 weeks)
Drama workshop	Tuesdays 7.15–9.15 (21 weeks)
Football training	Tuesdays 8.30–10 (21 weeks)
Introducing trampolining	Tuesdays 7.00–8.30 (11 weeks)
Looking at children's reading	Tuesdays 7.15–9.15 (4 weeks)
Mathematics to GCE O-Level	Tuesdays 7.15–9.15 (21 weeks)
Speak freely – for stutterers	Tuesdays 7.30–9.30 (11 weeks)
A study of two novels (*Middlemarch* and *Anna Karenina*)	Tuesdays 7.30–9.30 (11 weeks)
The traditional dances of England	Tuesdays 7.15–9.15 (5 weeks)
Volleyball	Tuesdays 7.00–8.30 (21 weeks)

Anyone for badminton? Want to play the guitar? Grow roses? Try the new mathematics? The titles of the courses themselves illustrate the breaking down of barriers which the Countesthorpe planners had in mind from the outset – barriers between school and home, between formal and informal learning, between educational, cultural, social and recreational motives.

Dances, disco sessions, table tennis, billiards, etc. are centred on the recreation room which provides an attractive meeting-place for young people in the area. The policy is to leave them to look after themselves rather than to push them into organized activities. In fact, most of those who join the lunch-time, junior and senior clubs are either former pupils or still in attendance at the school. The response from 'outsiders', i.e. those who have had no previous connections with the college, has so far been rather disappointing, possibly because of the membership fee (£1.50) – or could it be because one or other of the staff tutors is usually on duty to see that things do not get out of hand?

It may be thought that most, or all, of the services and facilities offered on the Countesthorpe campus are already provided by LEAs elsewhere, and that apart from the greater cost effectiveness resulting from multiple and constant use of the 'plant', nothing much is gained by bringing them together in one place. The point is that elsewhere the pieces of the jigsaw are kept separate. Here they coalesce and begin to form a pattern.

It is the pattern of a new way of life. The high-minded ideas that underlie its constitutional fabric are based on faith in the ability of ordinary people to organize their own affairs and to make the kind of arrangements which suit them best within the limits imposed by an elective-authoritarian system of management and government. Elective-authoritarian because, as McMullen sees it, British democracy consists of periodically electing a parliament or a local council which then proceeds to govern in what is fundamentally an authoritarian manner. In effect, the only active part which the individual can play is to choose which set of governors he prefers. At the level of institutions – industries, hospitals, schools – the management system is almost universally authoritarian, he thinks.

The justification for this form of government is probably an unspoken élitism: only the few are capable of 'governing' or 'managing'. This over the last fifty years has been linked with a technocratic concern with economic and material efficiency rather than with human satisfactions; though with the increasing size of organizations the actual efficiency of the authoritarian management system has increasingly been questioned. It is probably true, too, that when the major problem of most individuals was to earn sufficient to live a reasonable life they were too exhausted by the hours worked to worry about much else. However, it is already apparent that in many countries, including this, a substantial majority of people can earn sufficient for their reasonable material needs without undue exhaustion – and, if we avoid disaster, this tendency will accelerate over the working life of the children who will be coming to this college.

In short, while the constraints imposed by policy making at the level of central, regional and local government have to be accepted, there is considerable latitude of choice and freedom of action at the institutional level. The fact that taxpayers and ratepayers have no effective say in the financial provision made for them in the educational services does not mean that they are impotent when it comes to deciding how to *use* these services. Similarly, the fact that the teacher's style is cramped by external examination requirements is no excuse for a slavish acceptance of them. As more and more people become involved with framing them, the easier it will be to see that regulations lay down guidelines rather than fixed routes. To be free is to know how to assert one's legitimate rights. In a sense, this knowledge is the essential business of any education worth the name. Given this, any man may say, with Hamlet, 'O God! I could be bounded in a nut-shell, and count myself a king of infinite space'.

Unlike the free school, which rejects any constraints that it finds irksome, the open school represents a compromise, content to work within the framework of the existing system. If it does not correspond exactly with Illich's description of a convivial institution it is certainly a good deal nearer to it than the schools with which most of us are familiar. At a time when talk of participatory democracy tends to be dangerously loose, the need is not so much for theoretical justifications as for practical demonstrations of its worth. The Countesthorpe model may not be perfect but at least it is in good running order and gathering momentum as it goes.

(b) Wyndham School, Egremont

History and geography have played some strange tricks in West Cumberland. Outside the holiday season you can still 'wander lonely as a cloud' in Ennerdale or along the road beside Wastwater to the foot of Great Gable as Wordsworth did in his boyhood. This side of the Lakeland fells – 't back o' beyond' they call it hereabouts – is too remote for all but the hardiest hill walker, a shaggy waste of peat hags and crumbled drystone walls. Travelling south from Carlisle, the bleak little towns along the coastal strip – Maryport, Workington, Whitehaven, Egremont – have a lost, disconsolate look, reminders of an industry based on coal and iron ore which has long ceased to be prosperous. Then, five miles further down the road, a surprise: the massive atomic research and power stations of Windscale and Calder Hall.

Hill farmers living in scattered homesteads, miners whose pits were worked out, scientists and technicians brought in from all parts of the kingdom to service the installations of the Age of Technology: how to knit these disparate elements together? This was the problem facing the authorities in 1960 when plans for a new comprehensive school for the area came under discussion. Socially, economically and in other respects, the catchment area was peculiar. With a rapid influx of population in and around Seascale, at that time little more than a village, the solution hit upon by the planners was as ingenious as it was imaginative. In a word, the new building was to be multipurpose and the site chosen for it was close to the town centre in Egremont.

Wyndham School, opened in 1964, is the next best thing to a school without walls. Such walls as it has are so low that a child can look over them. A public right of way runs through the premises and people are constantly passing on their way to and from the shops. The intimate links with the town are nicely illustrated by the library, originally an all-age school dating from 1908: one entrance is for the public, the other for the school, with a reference room in between which is common ground. The library staff serve both sides of the building. The same dual usage applies to the indoor swimming bath, which is reserved for pupils during school hours and open to the public at other times. Again, the theatre and concert hall used by the English and music teachers also provide facilities for social drama groups and the town band.

Similarly, the coffee bar and lounge provided for the use of sixth formers is at the disposal of adult classes and others in the evenings, and the youth centre is occupied by nursery play groups in the mornings. Wyndham works round the clock.

A novel architectural layout finds its expression in an equally novel school organization. Here there are no prefects, no fixed rules, no 11-plus, no streaming, no examinations until the end of the third year, no corporal punishment, no uniform, no academic dress, no house cups, no prizes, no speech day. Wyndham has no use for the trappings of the traditional secondary school. Deschoolers and died-in-the-wool reactionaries alike, one suspects, would find it a bit of an eye-opener.

As might be expected in view of their very different home backgrounds, the pupils exhibit a wide range of ability. The yearly intake includes an unusually large proportion of clever children, others who are slow learners and quite a few who can only be classed as backward. They come from eleven primary schools, six of which are in small villages. On arrival, they spend their first year in the reception house, the idea being to ease the transfer to the secondary stage proper, after which they are allocated to one of eight houses. Each house has its own building, including dining and recreation rooms, and is designed to accommodate not more than 140 pupils. Six of the houses are reserved for children from rural schools, thus enabling members of the same family or from the same village to keep together. Children from the larger urban primary schools are dispersed among the other two houses, but each child has the right to nominate a friend to be placed with him.

Socially, the house is the unit for administration, meals, recreation, discipline, reports and links with the home. The head of house has personal contacts with 80 per cent of the parents, and progress reports on each pupil are issued at least twice each term. Each house has its own council and year committee.

Broadly speaking, all pupils follow a common course during the first three years, which corresponds to the French *cycle d'observation*.

Because of our great range of ability we have moved cautiously towards 'unstreaming' [the headmaster explains]. In 1964 we made 'bands' of ability containing only two forms each; in 1965 we had four in the top band and since 1968 there have been six parallel 'upper forms' in the year with either two or three, also parallel, taking the slowest children. Some setting is gradually introduced but we hope to keep this general organization three years. After all the pupils have taken French in the first year, Russian or German is added by some in the second.

At the fourth form stage the 'option system' maintains many sets of mixed ability. We try to defer as long as possible the choice between GCE and CSE, though certain sets aim specifically at one or the other from the beginning of the fourth. We fend off early specialization by teaching science to almost everybody below the sixth (and denying Latin to any but the few who need it for university: they take it up in the fifth form).

Set apart from the rest of the school in a separate building is the sixth-form college. Unlike the typical sixth form, it is fully comprehensive, including Oxbridge candidates as well as those who have yet to take their CSE examination. The proportion staying on to the sixth-form stage, 40 per cent, is considerably higher than the national average, and the numbers continue to grow. Here the sixth form is to a great extent self-governing and the policy is to leave it to work out its own salvation.

'We have abandoned completely the policy, once fairly common in some English schools, of keeping the school separate from the outside world of adults, worldliness and sin,' says the headmaster. With so many passers by – old folks sunning themselves on garden seats under the classroom windows, children playing on the lawns – Wyndham keeps open house for all concerned. Its affairs are as open to view as goldfish in a bowl. Where education as a continuous process ceases to be an empty phrase any formal distinction between 'learning' and 'living', 'school' and 'community' disappears. Their interrelationship is symbolized in the staff common room where teachers, librarian, youth counsellor and further education tutor are all members.

For thirty-six weeks in the year, the 'outside world' takes over the premises during the evenings, with 900 students enrolled for adult classes and very many more for a variety of social and recreational activities – young farmers' club, football club, consumer group, bridge club, political meetings, religious associations. Both the further education tutor and the youth counsellor are members of the daytime staff. All this helps to create an informal, friendly atmosphere in which there is no standing on ceremony, no place for pettifogging restrictions of role and status. Just as the public feels free to look in, the school feels free to look outwards. Some of its pupils help the aged, the handicapped and the needy in the area. Visits are paid to the old people's home and every year a variety of public functions is organized to raise money for school purposes and for charity. A summer fair, usually with a display of children's work, is patronized by as many as 4,000 parents and local people.

Wyndham School does not count its successes in terms of academic or athletic prowess. Its vision of the good life is proclaimed by the legend inscribed on its entrance.

> This school is dedicated to the brotherhood of all men and to the infinite possibilities of the spirit which is in them, to freedom from oppression and from prejudice, to the open mind and to the open door. On the wall appear names of men and women of our time who have championed one or other of these causes.

The list of names, to which new ones are added from time to time, includes Albert Schweitzer, Pope John XXIII, Gandhi, John F. Kennedy, Albert Luthuli, Helen Keller, Martin Luther King, Dag Hammerskjold and Bertrand Russell. It would be hard to think of worthier sponsors.

(c) 'What kind of a nut-house is this?'

'What's different about Adams?'

'Freedom – that's by far the most important thing. Around here I don't feel like I'm in jail.'

The context of this snatch of dialogue might be anywhere – Summerhill, say, or Countesthorpe, or Wyndham, or Scotland Road, Liverpool, or for that matter the school in the next street. In fact, it is taken from the front cover of *Phi Delta Kappan: a Journal for the Promotion of Leadership in Education*, which devoted its May 1971 issue to a series of feature articles outlining the rationale for a new kind of American high school.

For British readers, the main significance of the John Adams experiment is to be found in the manner in which it was brought about. Hard to imagine M.Ed. or Ph.D. candidates in one of our institutes of education banding together as an action group to plan the school of their dreams: harder still to imagine them ever being given the chance to implement such a plan. This is one dimension of freedom which British teachers serving in the state system have rarely or never dared to contemplate. Not so in the USA. In 1967,

Robert Schwartz and six other young teachers were in their final year of study at the Harvard Graduate School of Education. Impressed by the variety of functions simultaneously discharged in a teaching hospital – care of patients, training of interns, retraining of general practitioners, basic and applied research – they wanted to plan a clinical secondary school that would be comprehensive in more senses than the usual one. The school was to serve a threefold purpose in providing (a) instruction for adolescents, (b) on-the-job experience for university and college student trainees in teaching and social work, and (c) a research and development centre for curriculum projects, assessment and evaluation.

Evaluation, indeed, was the keystone of the group's plan which expressed itself in five straight questions for teachers:

(1) In what ways do you want people (particularly students) to be different after their contact with you than they were before?

(2) What would you be willing to accept as evidence that you had succeeded?

(3) What would you regard as undeniable evidence that you had failed and therefore should make changes?

(4) How might you go about gathering these kinds of evidence?

(5) How can you gather evidence in a way that will be meaningful to someone else?

On the answers to these questions, it was felt, the wholesome school climate which the group wished to create would depend.

Once formulated, the group's detailed proposals were sent off to several metropolitan school districts throughout the USA on the offchance that one of them might be interested. Portland, Oregon, gave them the chance they had been looking for.

John Adams High School opened in September 1969 in the midst of a racial flare-up. Its 1280 students – 25 per cent of them black – came from working-class and lower-middle-class backgrounds. They were randomly assigned to four 'houses', each having a complement of some 320 and its own team of teachers who remained responsible for them from grades 9 to 12. Working alongside the teachers, other members of the team included a guidance counsellor, a supervisor, an administrative *aide* and several college interns. Each of these house teams made its own arrangements and went its own way regardless of what the others might be doing. The team met half of its students for ninety minutes each morning and the remaining half in the afternoon, the rest of the day being set aside for elective courses and independent study. The organization of these house sessions was singularly adventurous, taking no account of age, ability and aptitude: a common course with a vengeance. Blockhead or genius, blue-stocking or dumb blonde – all were to receive the same treatment. However, in order to compensate for any loss in formal attainments and to allow for closer attention to individual differences ('getting to know you') Adams teachers had less scheduled time in the classroom than teachers in other Portland schools. Senior members of the staff held joint appointments as assistant professors of education at universities and liberal arts colleges in or around the city of Portland, and were engaged in curriculum projects, research and development as well as in the training of teachers.

Anyone familiar with the School Council's Humanities Project will discern a certain affinity with the central experiment in cur-riculum at John Adams High School. Race relations, slum clear-ance and urban renewal, air and water pollution, the Vietnam war, computers, automation, unemployment – these are typical topics discussed.

The general education program does not imply a throwback to the core curriculum of the progressive era [argued Allen L. Dobbins, one of the original members of the Harvard group, when he was head of the instructional division at John Adams]. Instead, we are attempting to develop an interdisciplinary, problem-solving curriculum, using disciplines as vehicles for studying these questions. Each discipline represents a syste-matic and structured form of thinking, and although there is overlapping, one asks different questions and seeks different information, depending on whether one is 'doing' history, political science or anthropology on the one hand or collecting and analysing scientific data on the other. Our intent is to draw upon the disciplines, and indeed to study them in con-siderable depth as they individually contribute to the study of a general education problem. An important goal of general education is that students learn characteristic processes of thinking unique to the different academic disciplines[1].

During one half of the school day, students may attend special classes, take part in a wide variety of elective courses (with or without supervision), take part-time jobs as apprentices, or even play hooky – 'goofing off' in American parlance. Students elect their own senate which acts as a decision making body and meets on an equal footing with the faculty senate. Joint committees representing both bodies meet regularly to discuss issues concerned with the curriculum, grading and any matters which are of direct concern to students and teachers. Although the principal retains the right of veto, the student and faculty senates are empowered to override him by a two-thirds majority vote if it comes to a showdown. In other words, the school's system of government is modelled on the American Constitution, a democracy which concedes not only a wide measure of freedom and responsibility to its members but also a fair measure of 'student power'.

Not surprisingly, a school organization which was prepared to go to these lengths for the sake of promoting harmonious teacher-pupil relationships soon found itself in trouble. At one of its early meetings the student senate caused a public outcry by refusing to accept the gift of an American flag from that most redoubtable of all donors, the Daughters of the American Revolution – a crime as heinous in the eyes of Oregonians as refusing to respond to the Loyal Toast is in the United Kingdom. Within two months a pressure group calling itself 'Citizens for a better Adams' was campaigning for the closure of the school. 'What kind of a nuthouse is this?' asked the leader writer of the local newspaper. Some parents complained bitterly that the education of their children was being neglected. 'Adams High does not teach respect for authority, discipline, basic scholarship, or orderly use of time. The school teaches gross egotism, extreme self-centredness, myopic self-delusion and general anarchy' said one – an opinion which might not have been taken quite so seriously had it not also been voiced by many of the students themselves. True, on the whole, most parents and pupils expressed themselves as being reasonably satisfied with the free-and-easy regime:

'I'm all for Adams. My daughter went to another high school for two years, but this is the first time she has taken the initiative to do studies and projects on her own.'

'We're learning to live with other races and other people here at

Adams. And all the math, English, Chaucer and history teaching in the past didn't teach our parents how to do that.'

'At my other school there were rules, rules, rules, rules all the time. Here it's so relaxed and nobody nags you.'

'I like the freedom – I can go where I want and I don't always have to be where somebody else tells me to go.'

Much more disturbing, however, was the discovery that a substantial minority wanted more positive direction from the teachers, more structured classwork, more attention to basic skills – in short, less freedom and more authority. Before the end of the first year, then, the experiment ran into difficulties which had not been foreseen at the start. It began to look like the old, old story of the lame man whose crutches had been taken away from him too suddenly. Neither pupils nor their parents were to blame if they were unready, unwilling or simply unable to accept the freedom which Schwartz and his team offered them. For those engaged in curriculum research and development the storm cones were well and truly hoisted.

Dissatisfaction became more acute and more widespread as the year progressed. Despite all the arrangements for a 'dialogue' between teachers and pupils, the latter rarely approached members of staff to air their grievances or discuss their problems – and those who did complained that nothing happened as a result.

Some students felt that they had become lazy or apathetic about their studies while attending Adams; some felt that they were learning less than they ever had before. And they admitted that they themselves had done very little to try to correct this; many found it impossible to overcome the temptation to simply drift. After all, nobody else seemed to worry about it – the teachers kept saying it was the student's decision to make. . . . The student who wanted or needed extremely implicit direction from teachers floundered. And although these students may have been relatively few in number, the impact of their disengagement on the school climate was serious. By spring 1970, it appeared to many of us that the school was characterized to far too great an extent by a pervasive restlessness and lack of commitment to the effort required to achieve excellence. Migratory bands of students in search of excitement looked in on classes, only to leave if what was going on was unentertaining.

Speakers were often treated embarrassingly rudely, films
were disrupted by chattering and rustling, and doors opened
to a stream of students who entered for a quick look and
departed for the next event promising diversion[2].

Critics who immediately jump to 'I told you so' conclusions
should be reminded that the record to date has not been one of
unmitigated disaster. On the contrary, the response from the
majority of students has been gratifying. No one denies that John
Adams High School is having a rough ride on the road to freedom
or that it has got as far as it has without taking some hard knocks
and suffering quite a few casualties. Some of the carefully framed
hypotheses in the group's original plan now begin to look like
hunches unlikely to pay off. In practice, it has not proved possible to cater for the entire spectrum of ability and interest in a
randomly assigned group without intellectual flabbiness resulting.
The vaunted interdisciplinary approach to general education has
turned out to be vastly more difficult than was anticipated, while
'problem-solving' has too often tended to mean discussions in
which nothing was concluded. Again, conditions of learning for
those who display neither ability nor interest have seemingly not
been enhanced by a permissive school climate. It is now realized
that readiness to shoulder the responsibilities which go with
self-discipline does not come easily, and may not come at all for
those who are unprepared for it: like learning to walk or learning
to read, it can be a painful business, at best halting, at worst ending in total collapse. Schwartz and his colleagues are the first to
admit the need for second thoughts, which is not the same as to
say that they are in any way less committed in principle to their
original plan. If they have learned anything, it is that there is no
single, allover pattern of general education to fit all shapes and
sizes of learner, that the formula for creating a stimulating school
climate is much more subtle and complex than they had supposed,
above all, that youngsters who cannot make good use of their
freedom will as often as not abuse it. The mistake was to imagine
that everyone would take to the new regime like ducks to water.

As Schwartz says:

The critical issues in secondary education have less to do with
free time and more with reordering the curriculum itself, and
with involving both teachers and students in the process. . . .

Admittedly we found it much easier to abolish hall passes, give kids more free time, and in general to create a reasonably humane climate than to figure out the essentials of a new curriculum. But without the kind of climate we are creating no curriculum would make much difference; the environmental issues must be dealt with before we can wrestle with the 'what knowledge is of most worth' kind of question[3].

In a sense, therefore, the 'climate' *is* the 'curriculum'. As a way of life, it has little or nothing to do with the formal content of the traditional secondary school whose supporters, naturally, find it empty and incomprehensible. To the extent that the values it upholds and the concept of learning it champions are not primarily intellectual it may be seen as the latest manifestation of the spirit of Jacksonian democracy which has always been strong in American life. But the tension between Jacksonian and Jeffersonian ideologies – egalitarianism and élitism, non-academic and academic motives – is permanent, and although peaceful coexistence between the two is not impossible more often than not it amounts to an uneasy truce. A school which has close links with the university on the one hand and with the local community on the other is bound to be a centre of conflict. The hope is that 'the university will keep the school intellectual and serious, and that the community will keep it relevant and honest'.

What's different about Adams? Enthusiasts have called it 'the greatest invention since sliced bread', 'the most carefully thought-out attempt to create a new kind of secondary school', and it has been described no less immoderately as a breeding ground for freaks and wastrels. Let its co-ordinator of research and development have the last word, then: 'As is true about much of Adams, we have not so much solved a problem as found out what the nature of the problem is.'[4]

References

1. Allen L. Dobbins, 'Instruction at Adams', *Phi Delta Kappan* (May 1971).
2. Patricia A. Werthemer, 'School climate and student learning', *Phi Delta Kappan* (May 1971).
3. Robert B. Schwartz, 'Profile of a high school', *Phi Delta Kappan* (May 1971).
4. Jerry L. Fletcher, 'Research and evaluation at Adams', *Phi Delta Kappan* (May 1971).

2 Degrees of freedom: time of one's own

(a) The Open University

The Open University has so far received less attention and less acclaim than it deserves from a public which prefers to wait and see. It might be different, of course, if this new foundation had a visible locus, say an imposing array of tower blocks enclosed in a lordly parkland estate, but what is the man in the street to make of a campus whose invisible domain extends from Alderney to Unst? Where are its crowds of students, its black and scarlet dons, its library, its halls of residence, its senate house? Useless to reply, 'Look around you', when there is little or nothing to be seen. In any case, what little can be seen bears no physical resemblance to the commonly accepted idea of a university.

First mooted as the 'University of the Air' by Harold Wilson in a speech in Glasgow in 1963, the venture has been nicknamed the 'university of the second chance' in the press, which may be taken as a compliment by its well-wishers or as a veiled slight by its detractors. In academic circles it has been received for the most part with polite indifference, if not with amused disparagement. Ideas about university education are so entrenched and their mystique so jealously preserved that no amount of advance publicity could dispel the suspicion that a university organized on these unorthodox lines was fated to rank second-best among its compeers.

Nevertheless, if only as a means of exploiting the possibilities opened up by modern networks of communication, it is no exaggeration to say that the Open University leads the world. By comparison, the planning of all the other post-Robbins foundations pales into insignificance.

Established in May 1969, its objectives are defined in the Royal Charter as:

> the advancement and dissemination of learning and knowledge by teaching and research by a diversity of means, such as broadcasting and technological devices appropriate to higher education, by correspondence tuition, residential courses and seminars and in other relevant ways; and to provide education of university and professional standards for its students and promote the educational well-being of the community generally.

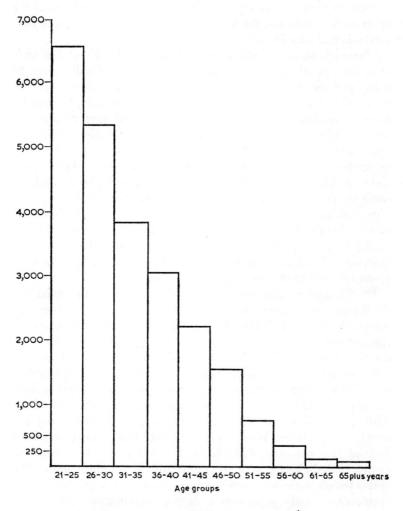

OPEN UNIVERSITY APPLICANTS AGE GROUPS *

*Based on first 23,698 applicants (percentages will not materially alter
in later figures)

Stripped of its sententious language, this means that it is a *national* institution – the Open University of the United Kingdom – open to people from every walk of life, open to places as far apart as the home and the television studio, above all open to new methods and new ideas.

There are no formal entrance requirements. Provided that he is over the age of 21 and can produce evidence of willingness to study and the necessary aptitude, the applicant does not need to have A-level or any other paper qualifications. Broadly, the admissions procedure operates on the principle of first come, first served. This does not mean, however, that early application necessarily secures registration. All applications are fed into a computer which has been programmed to ensure as far as possible a balanced distribution between geographical regions, occupational categories and the various foundation courses (arts, social sciences, science, mathematics and technology) offered for the BA degree. Plans are in hand for advanced postgraduate and professional studies, including the in-service training of teachers, but for the time being the main priority is given to work at the undergraduate stage.

Of the 42,000 men and women who wished to be registered for the first academic year beginning in January 1971, 25,000 were accepted – nearly half the intake of all the other British universities put together. (Anyone not accepted is placed on a reserve list on the understanding that he or she will receive favourable consideration the following year.) The number of applications varied from region to region, the largest proportion coming from the south-east. London, with an estimated 17.9 per cent of the adult population, was allocated 4,503 places; Scotland (9.3 per cent), 2,262 places. Wales (4.9 per cent) 892 places; Northern Ireland (2.7 per cent) 648 places. In most cases the allocations corresponded closely with the target quotas for the region. The male : female ratio was roughly 2 : 1. Less than 5 per cent of all applicants already possessed a degree qualification. The occupational groups ran the entire gamut from unskilled and semi-skilled (including unemployed) workers to administrators and managers. As might have been expected, the teaching profession (33 per cent) provided by far the strongest contingent, followed by members of the professions and arts (9.7 per cent), housewives (9.6 per cent), draughtsmen, laboratory assistants and technicians

(9.1 per cent), qualified scientists and engineers (9.0 per cent) and clerical and office staff (8.0 per cent). The initial response from working-class people – tradesmen, agricultural and industrial employees, etc. – was decidedly disappointing, no doubt because most of them had long since written themselves off as being incapable of university-level study, or because they were not sufficiently well informed about the opportunities and facilities offered and therefore unsure about what they might be letting themselves in for. An alternative explanation, of course, might be that they saw no point in gaining any sort of academic award. At any rate, it seems clear that the motive behind the vast majority of applications was the desire to improve the candidate's prospects of promotion – this despite the fact that the degree course was broadbased and designed to provide a general education. How many will eventually come to value it for its cultural, as distinct from its vocational, benefits must remain open to conjecture.

Analysis of applications and allocations for 1972 reveals no significant changes in the pattern of demand, except that the most frequently recurring age of applicants moved down from twenty-six to twenty-three, that fewer opted to take two foundation courses simultaneously, and that the total intake was reduced to 21,065. Once again, the response from unskilled and semi-skilled workers was so meagre that the university felt obliged to set aside a larger proportion of places than would normally be warranted by the number of applications from these occupational groups. In short, it begins to look as though recruitment may become progressively more of a problem once the backlog of applications from those who have narrowly failed to gain admission elsewhere shows signs of being exhausted.

Students do most of the work in their spare time, at home. In order to obtain a degree they must successfully complete six self-contained courses, two of them foundation courses, each lasting thirty-six weeks. Each course counts for a single credit. For candidates who wish to take the BA with Honours two additional credits are required. Exemptions from a foundation course may be granted to those who already possess an advanced qualification, e.g. HND, but the great majority who start from scratch can expect to spend anything from four to six years before graduating. They may, to be sure, take much longer: provided that they keep

This September, some of these kids will be out on the street.

If they're lucky.

That's right, lucky.

Each June, 500 students are chosen by lottery to be a part of the Parkway Program. At Parkway, an exciting, new experiment in high school education is taking place in the streets and offices of Philadelphia.

The Parkway Program is not a high school in the usual sense. Classes are not held in a schoolroom. School is not out by three.

Learning takes place 24 hours a day. On location. Journalism is taught at the offices of a major newspaper. Health services by a physician. Auto-mechanics class meets in an auto-repair shop. In all, students are free to choose from some 250 course offerings that lay the groundwork for college study in a unique and highly individual manner.

All of Philadelphia is our campus.

And it works. Parkway students mature faster. And learn more. Behavior problems have proved minimal. But the most impressive praise of all is that several other cities have already begun work on projects based on The Parkway Program.

So whether or not you know it, if you live in Philadelphia, you are part of the Parkway Program.

We want you to do more. Open your office, shop, or factory to these kids. Teach them something about your business. About the way you live.

In a time when the older generation seems to be losing touch with the young, we offer you a chance to make a meaningful contact.

It's up to you. We need you. But maybe not as much as you need us.

Send for more information. Send suggestions. Send offers of help. Or call. When these kids take to the street in September, they'll need you to guide them.

Parkway Program
c/o Franklin Institute
20th and Parkway
Philadelphia, Pa. 19103

up with their monthly assignments and pass the end-of-course examination in October they can make up their tally of credits as and when circumstances permit. Thus, married women who are having a baby or men who suddenly have to change their jobs and move to another part of the country may take leave of absence and resume their studies later on.

Higher education in Britain has always been, and remains, inordinately expensive. In terms of value for money, the Open University may well be the best buy on the market. Its total capital investment programme for the first five years of its existence, during which the number of registered students will be of the order of 80–100,000, will not exceed £6 million – compared with the £15–20 million needed to launch a conventional new foundation accommodating a mere 5,000 students. Instead of spending enormous sums on buildings, most of the money has gone into devising an instructional system which utilizes a unique combination of resources and techniques. The resulting savings benefit the student in two ways: first, by lowering the fees he has to pay, secondly, by offering him a package deal which must by any standard) be reckoned an extraordinarily good bargain. For the first-year foundation course the total charge is £45 – £10 on registration, £10 for tuition fees, £25 for the residential one-week summer school. (Most LEAs have agreed to foot the bill for the latter.)

In return, each student receives a monthly correspondence course package containing sets of reading material, work assignments, self-assessment exercises and tests which he has to complete and return – one set for each week during the thirty-six-week course. The package also includes timetables and background information concerning the television and radio programmes produced by the BBC in conjunction with the course planners. Viewing and listening to these is an integral part of the student's work, but occupies only a small fraction of his time: out of an estimated ten hours' study during any week he will be watching television for only twenty-five minutes. If he is a shift worker or lives in an area where reception is difficult or impossible arrangements are made for him to see or hear playbacks of the programmes at one of the 250-odd study centres throughout the country.

To help him, the student can call on the services of a counsellor, who acts as his adviser of studies, and is assigned to a course tutor, to whom he sends his written work for evaluation and critical comment. His progress is monitored by a process of continuous assessment. Most of the tests he has to complete are of the objective type, designed to be machine-scored and the results stored in a data bank. The self-assessment exercises which are built into the reading material enable the student to check his own progress, as do the regular reports he receives from his tutor and the computerized scores for his monthly tests. All this information forms part of a comprehensive feedback system, and its analysis serves to build up a 'picture' of the invisible student body, as well as assisting the course planners who are constantly seeking to improve the system.

Most of the work involved in the preparation, testing and full-scale production of course materials is carried out at Milton Keynes, Buckinghamshire, the university's administrative headquarters and its nerve centre. Here an academic staff comprising six faculties, together with experts from the university's Institute of Technology, authors, co-ordinators, editors, BBC producers and others join forces. The division of labour and responsibility in each of these course planning teams is too complex to describe briefly, but broadly speaking the academics (who come from several different disciplines) are concerned with the scholarly content of the course, the educational technologists with its structure, programming and testing, the authors, editors and producers with its presentation. Each contributes his particular expertise.

This is the much-vaunted 'multimedia approach' in action. Having decided what its instructional objectives are to be (which is not as easy as it sounds), the team has to review the available resources needed to achieve them. These resources can be baldly summarized as men, machines and materials. Print, television, radio, videotapes, sound recordings, experimental kits, apparatus, counselling, personal tutoring, summer-school seminars and discussion groups: what is the special contribution of each, what is the right 'mix', and how can they be fused into a meaningful whole? As regards print, which provides the bulk of the correspondence package, what kind of text will be best suited to an adult readership unaccustomed to private study? What further reading should be prescribed? Where, when and how can self-assessment exercises be written into the texts? What about the reliability and validity of the accompanying tests? How far can difficult concepts be elucidated by diagrams and illustrations? How can the learning experience be supplemented by television? By radio? Are course writers and producers perfectly clear about their terms of reference? Above all, how is the course related to the students' level of understanding, not to mention previous and subsequent courses which they may have taken or are due to take? These and a host of associated problems have to be thrashed out before any firm production schedule can be arranged. Course planning, in other words, follows a flow-chart procedure which is only made possible by the give-and-take between many minds, disciplines and skills.

Once the author has completed his first draft and submitted it for approval by the rest of the team, it is given a trial run with a sample of students who have volunteered their services as guinea-pigs. The data from this preliminary tryout are forthwith analysed by members of the university's Institute of Technology, which occupies a key position in the network and is responsible for the developmental testing of all courses. In nearly every case, the pilot run reveals deficiencies in the draft, which may have to be drastically revised. The revised version is then sent to an external assessor, usually an eminent authority in the field concerned, who checks it for any inaccuracies or factual errors which may have escaped the team's notice. The text is now ready for publication and the handling of it is left to the course co-ordinator, who is attached to the team from the start and acts as its liaison officer with the university's editorial, copyright clearance, media and graphics departments.

The task of reviewing and modifying courses proceeds continu-ously even after they have become operational. Unlike other institutions of higher learning, which remain curiously incurious about the effectiveness of their teaching methods (as the Hale Report noted), the Open University's policy is closely identified with research and development. The instruction it provides is intended to be self-correcting. It has to be.

Hitherto, the proponents of educational technology and cur-riculum development alike have done themselves, and their cause, a disservice by advancing claims which they were unable to fulfil. Too often their proposals have been couched in an arcane jargon which they did not always fully understand themselves – 'manage-ment of resources', 'behavioural objectives', 'systems thinking', 'schedules of reinforcement', and so on *ad nauseam* – a smoke-screen of theory behind which they took refuge rather than risk the indignity of failing in practice. If the educational technologist has sometimes appeared to be the devil in disguise as a human engineer, the would-be curriculum developer has figured as an ineffectual angel. For see what has happened in recent decades. First, programmed learning promised wonders, then Nuffield science, then closed-circuit television, then primary-school French, then computer-assisted instruction and for one reason or another each failed to live up to its promise. Everywhere, innovation or talk of innovation has been the order of the day, yet so far as most teachers, pupils and students are concerned, it has been a case of business as usual. Despite all the painstaking projects, all the research investigations and the countless working-parties, the rate of advance has been pitifully slow – 'about one mile a year' as the Earl of Leicester said of reforms in sheep-farming in the eighteenth century.

Although the educational technologist and the curriculum developer do not talk the same language they have a great deal in common, not least in being forward-looking. Both seek to extend and enrich learning experiences, to individualize the learning process, and to rationalize the use of manpower and material resources. It would be foolish to suggest that their efforts have been totally unavailing. In places they have met with some success, but as attempts to inject new life into the education system their impact has not been commensurate with the very considerable sums of money expended on them. To date, educational technology has *not* found ways and means of making teaching less labour-intensive. Curriculum development has *not* made any significant headway in the average classroom.

One reason for this sporadic progress stems from the lack of co-ordination between the various agencies engaged in this kind of enterprise. With here a project, there a project, everywhere a project, no concerted drive on a broad front has been possible. Any advances made have been in isolated sectors and intermittently. It is as though the machinery of innovation has been firing first on one cylinder, then on another, never in unison.

A second reason for this partial success – or near-failure, depending on the point of view – arises from the difficulty of grafting new techniques on to old or outworn institutions and organizations, difficulties no less acute in education than in the surgical transplanting of human organs.

Neither of these difficulties need affect the Open University. If applied systems theory calls for a combined operation in the grand manner it can provide just that. Like a new, science-based industry unencumbered by obsolete plant and inefficient methods of production, an institution of higher learning which can begin *de nouveau* like this has obvious advantages. That is why its advent is so charged with significance; and why, as it moves on to fortune, the indications are that it will come to be seen as the 'university of the first chance'.

But how well are its students faring? How many of them will stay the course? The history of educational reform is littered with the wrecks of excellent schemes which came to grief because they presupposed a taste for independent study which was not forthcoming in the long run. Even with the most carefully designed and attractive course materials, many adults, especially those who lack confidence in their ability to go it alone, are bound to find it difficult to do the work demanded by most academic disciplines. It is an illusion to suppose that there can be any soft options in the world of higher learning. The freedom to study at home in one's own way and in one's own time is easier to grant than it is to use.

The Open University is rightly concerned about the dropout problem. Of the initial intake of 25,000, roughly 9,000 had discontinued their studies by the end of the first year for one reason or other. Beyond the foundation-course stage, when the going gets more difficult, when counsellors and tutors tend to be stretched to their limit, a further decimation of the ranks has to be anticipated. Inevitably, many students with a job to hold down and a family to support find themselves hard put to it to keep up with their assignments. Weariness, distractions, isolation and fear of failure may discourage even the most resolute; support and advice cannot always reach them when it is most needed. A guidebook explaining how to study in a multimedia instructional system may be better than nothing, but in the absence of self-discipline it cannot really help. A preliminary get-together of students, counsellors and tutors, periodical visits to local and regional study centres, the annual summer school – all these foster the personal contacts and interchange of ideas that are

indispensable. The question is whether they are enough. For-
tunately, the network makes good use of the telephone. One of the
most promising developments, indeed, is the formation of study
circles by the students themselves. Meeting in private (or in
public) houses, these peer-matching groups may be seen as the
twentieth-century equivalent of the medieval *studium generale*,
only today they no longer find it necessary to sit at the feet of a
master. Such resourcefulness is heartening: one can only hope
that there will be more of it in the future.

More emphatically than the open school, the Open University
refuses to be fenced in physically, intellectually, ceremonially or
in other ways. Although its first graduates have yet to make their
appearance, it has already gone some way towards breaking the
monopoly of the traditional universities. So far so good, but in the
sense that it markets its wares mainly for a degree-hungry section
of the public, as distinct from honouring its pledge to 'promote
the educational well-being of the community generally', it has
done nothing, and looks like doing nothing to break the monopoly
of the licence to 'sell' academic awards. This licence has nothing
to do with the motives that make for lifelong learning: it is a
licence to print money, being the mechanism which enables
powerful vested interests to step up the supply of educational
services while at the same time boosting the demand for them, as
in any other growth industry.

> Just as manmade devices can first displace and then destroy
> nature, so systems, designed to service man, can first supple-
> ment and then subvert his natural ability to care for himself.
> Over-efficient production thus results not only in pollution but
> also in radical monopoly. By radical monopoly I mean the
> dominance of a type of product rather than a particular brand. I
> speak about radical monopoly when a production process
> exercises exclusive control over public resources by restricting
> the market to one commodity or profession. Cars shape cities
> in their image, ruling out locomotion on foot or bicycle. This
> is the danger, not the fact that more people may drive Chev-
> rolets than Chryslers. Schools monopolize learning by rede-
> fining it as 'education'[1].

At first sight it may seem positively ludicrous to suggest that
any university, let alone the Open University, keeps the student

so beholden to, and dependent on, its services as to 'subvert his natural ability to care for himself'. Until recently, the academic community has rarely given much thought to the need for pastoral care: provided that he paid his fees and refrained from any serious breach of regulations, no one saw anything wrong in leaving the student to sink or swim. Despite the university's claim to be a teaching institution, it was understood that whether he received a first, second or third class degree, or failed outright, depended far more on his own efforts than on those of his professor and the lecturing staff. Yet even where the discipline imposed was of the lightest – no compulsory attendance at lectures, no supervision of his private life, no interference with his political activities – the contractual relationship between the student and his university ensured that he remained subservient. The university was the only institution which could give him what he needed – not so much a liberal education, but the quasi-professional training that is the only recognized meal ticket in our meritocratic society.

The Open University's brand of higher education may be very different from the Oxbridge, Redbrick or Plateglass brands, yet it belongs essentially to the same type. In the present climate of opinion it could hardly do otherwise. It remains to be seen whether its packaged products will provide that service which is perfect freedom in the life of scholarship as it is in religion. In any case, it would be premature to forecast what will become of this lively 2-year-old. This much, at least, can be said in its favour, that unlike the Independent University, which seemingly plans to become even more exclusive and withdrawn from the common herd, the Open University does not restrict its instruction to its registered students. In time (who can tell?) its successes may be measured not so much in terms of the number of its graduates as by the size of its non-registered membership, the ones who feel free to take it or leave it and do not give a fig for caps and gowns and a piece of parchment. For them, too, 'it is all a purchase, all is a prize'.

Reference

1. Ivan Illich, unpublished paper (Centro Nationale de Documentacion, 1971).

(b) The Inter-University Biology Teaching Project

If a library is a storehouse for print, a resource centre might be called a storehouse for other media. From the one, a student may borrow a book on rugby football or a life of Beethoven; from the other (ideally) a loop film which shows him how to kick a drop goal or an LP record of the Ninth Symphony for him to listen to at his leisure. In practice, it is a good deal easier for him to borrow books than it is to gain access to audio-visual aids since resource centres are few and far between and neither so well stocked nor so well organized as libraries. Whatever his interest happens to be, he can usually count on finding the book he wants on the shelves, and if not it can be obtained for him on loan within a matter of days. Cataloguing makes for easy retrieval and there is always plenty to choose from. A public library, like a public park or for that matter a public house, is open to all – the kind of place where anyone is free to come and go whether it be for amusement or for more serious studies. There he can browse around and take his pick of what the storehouse offers. The same can hardly be said of most of the resource centres which are now springing up all over the country. After four centuries of Gutenberg technology, it is not surprising that the multimedia approach envisaged in the Open University has a long way to go before it overtakes and surpasses the nineteenth-century idea of the university as a collection of books. Carlyle's London Library started life in 1841 with a mere 3,000 volumes and now adds to its enormous collection at the rate of 8,000 new titles each year – and even this represents less than one-third of the output from British publishing houses alone. By comparison, resource centres are still at the stage of development of the chained library in York Minster which contained forty volumes in Alcuin's day. True, film libraries and record libraries have been with us for some time, but, on the whole, modern software, though equally portable, is not so convenient to handle as print, and discs, films, videotapes, cassettes and the rest are useless without the hardware that goes with them. Mechanical equipment is expensive, often cumbersome and apt to break down at critical moments – as when the lecturer finds to his chagrin that the three-pin plug for his slide projector does not fit the wall socket.

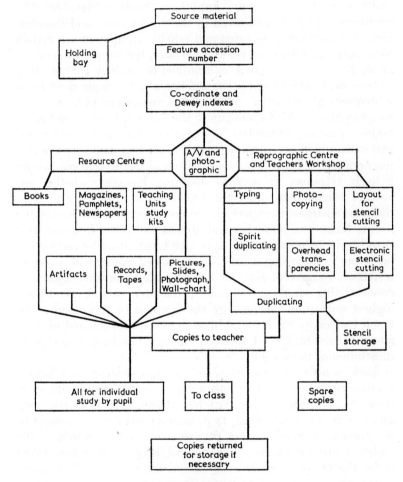

FLOW CHART
CODSALL COMPREHENSIVE SCHOOL

To be sure, software includes a whole list of resources other than those which come under the heading of audio-visual aids. The problem is to know how to assemble them so that they are easily accessible and, more important, easily retrievable. The engineering problems involved in the manufacture and distribution of cheap, easily operated and reliable equipment are certain to be surmounted sooner rather than later, but for the time being, as we have already argued, educational technology cannot claim to have made life easier for the teacher who has aspirations to be a 'manager of resources'. Most of the curriculum projects sponsored by the Nuffield Foundation, the Schools Council and other bodies provide exemplary supportive and self-instructional materials which are intended to serve as foundations on which teachers can build. In places, as at Codsall, these have sparked off a lively response. It remains doubtful, however, whether the average teacher has either the time or the skill to create from these foundations: to expect him to do so seems rather like asking him to be author, publisher and librarian all rolled into one. If it is to be viable, a multimedia approach must either be carried out on a big scale, using costly, sophisticated equipment – radio, television, computers, etc. – or it must settle for limited objectives, concentrating on the small-scale production of software of the highest quality and using only the simplest of equipment. The Open University has been taken as an example of the first of these alternatives. The Inter-University Biology Teaching Project is an illustration of the second.

Some 700 first-year science and medical students at Glasgow University are required to take a course in biology. Quite apart from the numbers, experience has shown that it is not very satisfactory, to say the least, to present a survey of the subject in the form of lectures, seeing that as many as two-thirds of the audience may be absolute beginners while others may have taken it for the O- or A-grade examination for the Scottish Leaving Certificate. Many need to be given an elementary introduction; others are ready to begin fairly advanced study. Yet all must reach a given standard of proficiency if they are to satisfy the examiners and continue with their degree course. To prescribe a textbook and leave them to get on with it would be unthinkable. To divide them into sets according to their different levels of understanding, and give lectures appropriate to each set might be tricky, not to say invidious, and in any case difficult to arrange; and if the same lectures are given to all the chances are that some students will find them virtually unintelligible, others so over-simplified as to be a waste of time.

To see how a problem so intractable in the lecture theatre has been solved in a drawing room one has only to step inside No. 22 Bute Gardens, a Victorian house which has been taken over by Glasgow University's Departments of Zoology and Education. Here for the past two years a small research and development team has been preparing a self-instructional module consisting of fifteen self-contained programmes on developmental biology. This is Glasgow's contribution to a joint project financed by the Nuffield Foundation in which five British universities are participating.

The immediate purpose of the module is to provide first-year undergraduates (ultimately sixth formers as well) with the basic facts, concepts, principles and theories concerning the development of animals and plants. The topics included cover, in order, (1) cells, (2) cells in action, (3) mitosis, (4) meiosis, (5) fertilization, (6) cleavage, (7) gastrulation, (8) mustering cells into organs, (9) morphogenesis in plants, (10) growth, (11) nucleus and cytoplasm, (12) hormones, (13) developmental switches, (14) shape and pattern, (15) embryos and larvae. Each of these programmes takes approximately 50 minutes to complete, though the actual time taken varies considerably from individual to individual. All students are given a diagnostic test to ascertain which of the pro-grammes they need to take. Although they are advised that it is in their own interest to make full use of the facilities there is no compulsion to do so: the house is open throughout the day and students are free to come and go as they please – or to stay away altogether. They can drop in for half an hour during the lunch break or spend the whole morning and afternoon there, according to their personal inclination.

On entering the building, the student selects a card bearing the number of the programme he is working on and clocks in, helps himself to the materials he wants from the storeroom, then takes his seat at one of the twelve booths in the adjoining drawing room. Here laid out on a desk are three items of equipment: (1) a filmstrip viewer, (2) a cassette player with a headset for listening to the recorded soundtrack, (3) a response sheet. The hardware is

easy to operate, practically foolproof and relatively inexpensive –
amounting to not more than £23 for each place.

These three items correspond to the three channels of communication of what is, in effect, a multimedia instructional
system. Biology lends itself to visual treatment, so most of the vital
information is displayed in the form of colour transparencies –
photographs, diagrams, drawings – which can be viewed in a
prearranged sequence (each frame is numbered) on the filmstrip.
The accompanying soundtrack supplies additional information as
well as the stimulus of the spoken word (the inflection, emphasis
and 'human interest' which are missing in the run-of-the-mill
programmed text), but its main purpose is to prompt the viewer,
drawing his attention to points of special significance, reminding
him what to look for. The soundtrack also poses questions. Whenever a question is asked the student switches off while he considers
his answer and writes it in his response sheet. To that extent, the
soundtrack may be said to control the pacing of presentation and
to provide immediate 'knowledge of results'. The response sheet,
which the student retains, summarizes the factual content of the
programme with supplementary information in the form of
diagrams, historical notes, definitions and references. Besides
being a means of self-assessment, the response sheet enables the
student to keep a permanent record of his work and can be
used for revision. If only because it is so carefully structured
and sequenced it is almost certainly more accurate and help-
ful as an *aide-mémoire* than the hastily scribbled notes and
occasional handouts on which the student has had to rely in the
past.

Needless to say, all the programmes have undergone a preliminary process of testing and revision. The early ones in the
series, being mainly factual, are meant to be self-explanatory and
the student's responses are largely a matter of recall: later on, they
demand a progressively higher level of conceptual thought and
problem solving. Thus, towards the end, the student is expected
to frame his own hypotheses and to suggest experiments for testing
these.

No particular time limit is set for the completion of the series.
Beginners who work through all fifteen programmes at the rate of
one per week may cover most of the ground in the course of a
single term: those who are more advanced at the outset and whose

performance on the diagnostic test indicates that they can safely skip numbers 1–4, say, may take only a few weeks.

Between 80–90 per cent of the target population have elected to try out the system since it became fully operational. To date, reactions have been extremely favourable: 'easy to use', 'more interesting', 'clear presentation' are some of the typically appreciative comments made by students who have never previously had an opportunity of learning for and by themselves and in their own time. While it is too early to decide whether or not this initial enthusiasm will last, it can be said that a system which requires a minimum of supervision is now a going concern and running smoothly.

As happens whenever a programmed format is introduced, there are striking differences not only in the rates at which individuals work, but also in the *ways* they use the system. One student may spend a whole morning laboriously copying all the diagrams and captions on the filmstrip into his notebook, regardless of the soundtrack and the response sheet. Another may return five or six times to work through the same programme again and again. Yet another may race through two or three programmes at a single session. Some leave it until late in the term before making a start: others plod along tortoise-fashion. As a result, there are times when most of the booths are unoccupied and times when the room is so full that newcomers are kept waiting. On the whole, however, serious dislocation has been avoided: hindsight, indeed, shows that within the limits set by numbers (2–300) and time (about 15 weeks) smooth running is perfectly possible with as few as eight sets of equipment.

One of the lessons learned from the project so far has been the need for prior consideration of the practical problems of usage. By applying queue theory, the course planner should be able to give his colleagues a clear indication of the requirements before the programme's objectives are determined, so that the conditions for achieving maximum utilization are observed from the outset. In situations where reliable, self-instructional hardware is involved, cost effectiveness only becomes feasible if programmes are designed for use at high traffic densities. In this particular instance the management of the flow of traffic has been left more or less to chance without incurring any serious loss in efficiency – after all, a self-instructional system capable of dealing with 2–300 students at a cost of less than £600* may be accounted a notable saving in manpower and money even if there are occasions when the equipment is left idle – but the management techniques at the disposal of the course planners will certainly play their part as the project proceeds. So, too, will the knowledge gained from the analysis of the clocking-in cards from which a detailed breakdown of every student's progress can be obtained and checked against his eventual performance in the end-of-year examination. As with all courses which follow a systems approach, this one is designed to be self-correcting.

As described here, the system operates on a library basis, but it is flexible enough to allow of a variety of usages. The lightweight equipment, programmes and all, can be carried in a briefcase and used at home if need be. Alternatively, it can be used in the normal classroom situation with a lecturer or a teacher present to control the pacing and lead the discussion. Research experience at Glasgow University suggests that group presentation is probably as effective as self-instruction but not so popular with the students. Again, small groups of up to six students may use the programmes as the basis for unsupervised discussion groups.

(*Module 1: Developmental Biology* is to be published by Longman, together with the diagnostic test, post-tests and a teacher's manual containing suggestions on how to use it most effectively and how it can be integrated with existing courses.)

3 A place of one's own

(a) Free Schools and Little Schools in Denmark

In the history of educational thought the name of N. F. S. Grundtvig is as illustrious as that of Sören Kierkegaard in existentialist philosophy. Poet, priest, scientist and cultural revivalist, Grundtvig is chiefly remembered as the *fons et origo* of the Folk High School movement which has spread far beyond his homeland and which indirectly helped to inspire and influence the planning of the Cambridgeshire Village Colleges. As the instigator

* 5 sets of programmes at £50 per set, 12 places at £23 per place: total cost = £526.

of a protest movement on behalf of free schools he is rather less well known.

Grundtvig hated the arid formalism of the traditional secondary (Latin) schools of his time, which he castigated as 'schools for death' and 'houses of correction'. Like Rousseau, he affirmed the need for a developmental approach and regarded the practice of 'stretching' the young learner's intellect as premature and damaging. He was bitterly opposed to compulsion in any shape or form, not least to compulsory denominational religious instruction. As Rousseau found a worthy disciple in Pestalozzi, so Grundtvig found his in Kristen Kold, who founded the first Free School (*Friskole*) in 1852.

For administrative purposes, the term *Friskole* covers a wide variety of private schools in Denmark. According to the official publication, *Schools and Education in Denmark* (Det Danske Selskab, 1964), there are more than 270 of them, but it appears that the numbers are actually declining, for the latest information from the Ministry of Education indicates that only 162 were recognized for state and municipal subsidy in 1969–70. In 1964 it was estimated that they accounted for some 7 per cent of the total school-age population, whereas at present they account for slightly less than 5 per cent; 30,773 pupils as against 558,179 enrolled in publicly maintained schools. Most of them are in rural or suburban areas. By no means all of them are of the Grundtvig-Kold type and since the 1930s a new kind of 'protest' school, usually referred to as the Little School (*Lilleskole*) has shown signs of becoming increasingly popular. For all practical purposes the names Free School and Little School are interchangeable. Broadly speaking, the reasons for wanting to opt out of the state-controlled system are much the same in Denmark as they are in other countries, but having said that, any resemblance between these Free and Little Schools and the independent sector in Britain may be thought to end. Their ethos is entirely different. Some inkling of the difference may be gathered from a poem which appeared in the August 1966 issue of *Den Frie Laerer-Skole*:

Your children are not your children.
They are the sons and daughters of Life's longing for itself.
They come through but not from you,

And though they are with you, yet they belong not to you.
You may give them your love but not your thoughts,
For they have their own thoughts.
You may house their bodies but not their souls,
For their souls dwell in the house of tomorrow, which you
   cannot visit,
Not even in your dreams.
You may strive to be like them, but seek not to make them like
   you.
For life goes not backward nor tarries with yesterday.

Although education is compulsory in Denmark, parents are not
obliged to send their children to a publicly maintained school, or
to any sort of school for that matter. Under Section 76 of the
Constitution they may opt for home tuition provided that the
standard and type of instruction is 'comparable' with that which
is normally required in the state system. In that event, all they
need to do is to notify the local school board (in Copenhagen the
school directorate), stating the names and ages of the children
concerned, the address at which they are to be found, and who is
to be responsible for teaching them. Parents whose qualifications
and experience are deemed to be adequate may even be exempted
from inspection and supervision by the authorities. As might be
expected, however, very few avail themselves of this constitutional right and only one out of every 3,000 Danish children
receive their education at home. On the other hand, the right
which enables common-interest groups of parents to organize
and manage their own schools and to have them recognized for
grant purposes is widely exercised.
   Legally, Free Schools are defined as 'private schools which give
instruction to their pupils throughout the whole period of compulsory education and which provide instruction comparable
with that which is normally required in the *Folkeskole* [state-
provided school]'. Apart from this, there are no preconditions for
establishing them, beyond notifying the authorities of their existence. If it wishes, a Free School *may* place itself under the supervision of the local authorities, but if it is owned and controlled by
a board of managers or has an influential parents' committee –
influential in the sense that the committee is representative and
has an effective say in the school's affairs – it is entitled to nomi-

nate its own local supervisor. In any case, supervision is only concerned to ensure that reasonable standards of attainment in the 3 Rs are maintained, that attendance is regular, and that the accommodation is hygienic. No requirements are laid down regarding the number of days or weeks in the year in which the school is to be kept open, the methods used, or the scope and content of the curriculum. Normally, a Free School does not prepare its pupils for any state-controlled examination.

Provided that these minimal conditions are satisfied, a Free School is eligible to receive state aid in the form of an 85 per cent subsidy for the following expenditures: (1) teachers' salaries, (2) upkeep of premises, (3) heating, lighting, power supply and cleaning, (4) taxation and insurance, (5) rent of premises, playground and open-air areas, (6) interest on loan mortgages on school property and (7) other incidental expenses. In addition, it receives a 50 per cent *per capita* grant for its pupils. Before it can be recognized, the school must have enrolled fifteen pupils for the previous three years, but if it has been receiving state subsidies for a period of several years this number may be reduced to as low as ten. Not for nothing are they called Little Schools.

Some Free Schools seek to perpetuate the Grundtvig–Kold tradition. Others cater for sectarian interests – Roman Catholic, Jewish, Seventh Day Adventist and ecumenical – or, as in South Jutland, for German-speaking minorities. There are also private *Realskoler* which prepare pupils for university entrance and Free Youth Continuation Schools, mainly residential, for school-leavers between the ages of fourteen and eighteen, but in general it may be said that the Free and Little Schools with which we are here concerned cover the primary and middle-school stages and that their outlook is markedly progressive.

While the law does not require any particular religious or political affiliation, it seems that in the nature of things the Free or Little School must have its own ideological *raison d'être* and that in most cases this is a genuine concern for the quality of education. The criticism that they pander to upper-middle-class sectional interests is stoutly resisted by the claim that they represent groups of parents who care intensely about the upbringing of their children and who are entitled to think that they can establish schools which are superior in many respects to those provided for them by the authorities. A more humane atmosphere, closer links between school and home, greater involvement on the part of parents, mutual give-and-take between parents and teachers, a more informal extended family type of organization, more opportunities for old and young to engage in shared experience – these are some of the reasons advanced to justify their existence. Other arguments urged in their favour are that these schools pay more attention to creative, aesthetic and group activities, that the emphasis on the acquisition of cognitive skills is relaxed, and that the spirit of competition is replaced by healthy co-operation. In the judgement of Dr J. Munch-Peterson, deputy head of the International Relations division of the Danish Ministry of Education:

> Advanced methods of teaching are tried out, and most teachers interested in and engaged in teaching in the Little Schools are young teachers who also try out new forms of personal and close association with their pupils, pupil participation in laying down disciplinary regulations, and in types of educational activities to be taken up. Most of the new schools of this type are situated in new suburban areas inhabited by young parents[1].

An American observer with no axe to grind notes that:

> the educational milieu tends to be fairly permissive and informal, with a heavy emphasis on creativity in the arts and a stress on the development of co-operation and humanitarianism. These schools are based on the principles that pupils must be allowed a great deal of democratic freedom, that the students ought to play as active a role in the educational process and the running of the school as the teacher, that creativity be emphasized, and that parents play an active part in the daily workings of the school[2].

Some idea of the philosophy underlying the Little School movement and of how it translates itself into everyday practice may be ascertained from an interview with Rasmus Hansen, headmaster of Gladsaxe *Lilleskole*:

> Q. Is it not undemocratic that privileged parents' children should have their own schools and enjoy special privileges instead of mixing with other children?
>
> R.H. That's a question which has worried us for many years but I don't think that it should cause us too much concern.
>
> Q. How big ought a Little School to be?

R.H. Here in Gladsaxe we believe the limit to be around 100. As teachers, it is vital to have a democratic foundation for our work, to show that we can talk about our problems freely, co-operate with other people paying due regard to different points of view.

Q. Isn't it true that the children you have here are from upper-class backgrounds?

R.H. Our children belong mainly to the middle classes. We have none with very high incomes, but on the other hand there are none from the lower income groups.

Q. What is the cost of sending a child to your school?

R.H. 113 Kroner per month for the first child; 81 Kroner for the second and 54 Kroner for the third.*

Q. Would you like to say something more about the parents?

R.H. Yes, in particular as regards their co-operation with the school. Parents come here very frequently. We hold joint meetings to discuss matters of mutual interest and to make plans. We hold classes in which parents work alongside their children. Parents are active in committees, in publishing the school newspaper, in taking children on excursions, etc. They join in camps, nature trails, Christmas parties, that sort of thing. Sometimes they serve as teachers; occasionally they may even take over for a whole day while the staff goes off to discuss their work in peace and quiet.

Q. Anything else?

R.H. We think it most important that parents and teachers together should set an example. This is essential if we are to preserve a democratic outlook. In other words we must be able to talk to each other, work together, resolve our problems between ourselves and show that we respect and understand other people's needs.

Q. What about the curriculum?

R.H. The children learn Danish by writing stories and poetry, by telling stories, by acting plays and running their own newspaper. They learn to write by writing. In this way we aim to make reading, writing and other subjects genuinely creative. To create entirely on one's own not only gives pleasure but provides a means of contact with others.

* Roughly £8, £5 and £3 respectively.

Q. Do your children's parents all share the same outlook on
   life?

R.H. As regards religion and politics, no, but they have all near
     enough the same attitude towards the upbringing of
     children. Among other things, they believe that a secure
     and harmonious development offers the child the best
     chance of discovering himself as a person in later life[3].

Further comment would be impertinent: any evaluation of the
effectiveness, desirability and quality of the education provided in
these Little Schools is better left to the Danes. But even in a small
agricultural country their contribution to the national life may be
accounted relatively insignificant. Fairly clearly, they are more
popular among professional, managerial and well-to-do parents
than they are among those of working-class origins who do not
care to avail themselves of their constitutional rights or are prevented from doing so for financial reasons. For the comparative
educationist, however, the Danish arrangements for facilitating
the ownership and control of schools are not without interest.
Since 1870 both the central and local authorities in Britain have
shown themselves to be extremely reluctant to grant recognition,
let alone subsidize, private-venture establishments: indeed, the
effect of national policy has consistently discouraged them,
stressing parents' duties at the expense of parents' rights. Increasingly, these 'duties' have come to be interpreted as an obligation
to send children to state-provided schools, while 'rights' have been
whittled down to a Hobson's choice against which there is little
or no appeal. As schools have grown bigger, and as the costs of
building, equipping and maintaining them have escalated, any
effective rights have been reserved, with few exceptions, for the
wealthier classes and any possibility of free enterprise has been
almost eliminated. While recognizing that administrative arrangements which meet with approval in one national system may not
be applicable in another, it is difficult to avoid the conclusion that
the British system is more concerned to place obstacles in the
path of free enterprise than it is to remove them. Certainly, it
appears that it is a good deal easier to start a school of one's own
in Denmark than it is in this country, if only because the financial
assistance offered is vastly more generous. As a model, the Free
or Little School may not be for export: all the same, as a demo-

cratic and humane alternative to state-provided schooling, its
attractions and its possibilities are not to be denied.

References

1. J. Munch-Peterson, in litt.
2. Estelle Fuchs, 'The Free School of Denmark', *New York Saturday
   Review* (August 1969).
3. Den lille skole- en produktiv skole', *Den Frie Laerer-Skole* (August
   1966).

(b) School for Scousers

The Scotland Road–Vauxhall district of Liverpool is a classic
example of an urban-industrial community which, rightly or
wrongly, considers that it has been ill-served by an education
system apparently insensitive to its needs. It exhibits all the
characteristic features of an educational priority area – poverty,
congestion, bad housing, high rates of unemployment, truancy
and juvenile delinquency, low levels of aspiration and expectation;
and it is against this background that the initiatives of the Scotland
Road Community Trust, formed in the late autumn of 1970, have
to be seen. Perhaps only a kitchen-sink novelist or a *Love on the
Dole* dramatist could do full justice to the tragicomedy of the
Trust's earliest efforts. Operating on a shoestring budget, it
began by organizing five-a-side football matches between the
frequenters of local pubs and followed up by arranging cut-price
camping holidays for youngsters in the summer, providing food
hampers for old-age pensioners and parties for homeless and
lonely people at Christmas. Next it acquired a battered old
laundry van which was used for low-cost house removals and
collecting unwanted furniture for distribution to those in need.
The Trust was, and remains, entirely dependent on voluntary
subscriptions, most of them raised in the locality. Raffles, sweep-
stakes, jumble sales and donations ranging from a packet of nails
to the loan of a cottage in North Wales helped to keep it going on a
hand-to-mouth basis during the long hard months pending its
recognition as a registered charity. Soon it had plans for converting
a plot of waste ground into an adventure playground, for converting a derelict warehouse into a discotheque-cum-youth-club,

and for using its 'fleet' of vehicles – box van, ambulance and 12-seater mini-bus – for soup runs, local transport and trips into the countryside. Finding garage space was a problem and one or other of the vehicles was usually off the road because the money needed for repairs, licencing or MOT tests was simply not available, but somehow the make-do-and-mend philosophy of those engaged in the Trust's activities sustained them in the face of these temporary setbacks.

The Scotland Road Free School opened its doors in June–July 1971, beginning with 5 children and ending with 16. It reopened in the following September with 30 pupils, housed in the Everton Red Triangle Club belonging to the YMCA, later in a church hall. The venture immediately attracted the interest and attention of the news media; understandably, too, for here at long last was a breakaway movement which seemed to British ways of thinking singularly bold, not to say defiant. That the upper and middle classes could assert their rights to organize schools had always been taken for granted, but for an impoverished subculture to opt out of the statutory system was, to say the least, unexpected.

The prospectus of the Free School was at once uncompromising and decidedly sketchy.

> The school will be a community school which will be totally involved with its environment [it announced in the preamble]. The nature of this involvement will be such that the school will be in the vanguard of social change in the area. By accepting this role, the school will not seek to impose its own values, but will have as its premise a total acceptance of the people and the area. It is felt that the organization of education is insensitive, unaware and in content largely irrelevent [sic] to the needs of the children and their future roles as adults in the society. Particularly in the Scotland Road–Vauxhall area, it has not provided for the aspirations, life and culture of the people, who have a social heritage worthy of itself which must be given an identity and expression of its own. We do not seek to alienate people from their backgrounds, but seek to enrich and intensify their lives.

For those who were curious to know how the school was to be organized the prospectus, such as it was, gave some forthright answers:

Q. *What is a free school?*

A. A free school is a different kind of school which is controlled by parents, children and teachers together.

Q. *What is meant by 'free'?*

A. Of course you do not have to pay, but free means here that the community controls the school and not the education authority.

Q. *What are the advantages of a free school?*

A. Some of the advantages are as follows.

Due to its small size the school can cater more directly for the needs of each child.

The school will be all-age and family groups will be able to attend together.

The school can adapt itself to the needs of the community. This means that the school and its equipment can be used during holiday periods for play groups etc., and in the evenings by any local association.

Q. *Can I send my children to the school?*

A. Yes.

Q. *Will religion be taught in the school?*

A. Facilities will be offered to any priest wishing to come into the school.

Q. *Can my children do examinations at the school?*

A. Yes. Provision will be made for any child wishing to sit external examinations such as CSE or GCE.

Q. *When enrolled will attendance be compulsory?*

A. Yes. The law requires that children will attend.

Q. *Will lessons be compulsory?*

A. No. We believe that children learn best when stimulated through interest.

Q. *Will the school have a headmaster?*

A. No. In the school everyone has an equal voice in the school council.

The reasons given for wanting to establish a Free School are broadly the same as in Denmark, and may be adjudged sound. Some of the more bombastically phrased assertions seem to lose touch with reality. At least some of the alleged advantages – e.g. that the school and its equipment can be used during holiday periods for play groups etc. – if they are not altogether spurious,

can be claimed with equal or better justification by many local
education authority schools. As for the assurance that pupils who
intend to become candidates for a leaving certificate will not be
handicapped, sceptics may query whether that means anything at
all. Indeed, it is difficult to see these proposals having any great
appeal to the average working-class parent who may be forgiven
for failing to find them convincing. They are addressed, obviously,
to a disaffected minority. Informed opinion will be inclined to
dismiss them as the fulminations of a lunatic fringe. Without
adequate financial backing, without official recognition and without any of the safeguards that are usually thought necessary for
the organization and maintenance of schools, the new venture
could hardly have got off to a more precarious start in life. Still
less than six months old, the odds against its succeeding seem
heavy, yet the very fact that it has aroused such widespread
comment and speculation is one indication of a latent goodwill
which may eventually rally to its support. If the strange goings-
on in a draughty church hall have caught the public interest
it is because of a sneaking sympathy for the underdog. Bizarre
happening or the opening scene in an educational drama the
like of which we have not seen in our lifetime – which is it to
be?

By the end of its first term the Free School had enrolled
40 pupils whose ages ranged from six to sixteen. The original
estimate of a 50 pupil intake had been made in the belief that the
school would quickly be oversubscribed, but to date the response
from parents and children alike has been understandably cautious.
Although chronically short of cash, the Trust has ambitious plans
for renting a larger and more suitable building at an annual cost of
£5,000, but for the time being these are necessarily in abeyance.
It cannot afford to pay its full-time workers, most of whom draw
social security. The teachers live in the area, five of them on the
premises, dossing down in sleeping bags on the floorboards. 'We
never close' is one of their proudest boasts. Several of them are
graduates who say that they have tried teaching in local authority
schools and found it a distasteful experience or in some way
unrewarding. Roughing it, mucking in and not standing on
ceremony is expected of everyone who offers to help. As in other
communes, the group is non-hierarchical and recognizes no
authority.

It is a bit difficult to put into words and the theory is ahead of the practice [writes Andrew Churchill, one of the members]. What happens is that no one has just one role. If someone arrives to join us they are not given any specific duties and so do not have a 'comfortable' role, as with almost all other jobs. Instead, each person finds out what needs to be done and what possibilities there are and then goes ahead with whatever tasks he thinks he wants to do. We make very little distinction between work and leisure – we just live. This brings a great many benefits and also some problems. One of the benefits is the sheer enjoyment in what we are doing (although this is tied up with the fact that we are doing what we want to do). Another is that a great deal more seems to get done.

Inevitably, the ménage seems slightly Micawberish. Not so much a school, more a play centre, most casual observers would say. The school is provisionally registered as an independent school with the Department of Education and Science and was barely into its stride before it came under the scrutiny of Her Majesty's Inspectors. What they saw must have left them sorely puzzled. Arriving at 9.30 a.m. to find that none of the pupils had turned up was hardly the kind of reception to which they were accustomed; and what were they to think on being informed that no one kept a register? Who, then, was in charge? No one in particular, apparently. Could they see the library? Sorry, there was none. Timetable? None. Schemes of work? None. Some examples of work done by the children, perhaps? Only a scattering of lurid watercolours on the walls. If not exactly a non-event, the visitation seems to have been embarrassing on both sides: a case of cross-cultural shock, one might say. The usual civilities were observed and there was a 'useful exchange of views', as the politicians say in their communiqués, after which the inspectors made a discreet withdrawal. What they made of it all is easily conjectured.

As an 'alternative school for Liverpool', the Free School is nothing if not unconventional. Although informal in organization it is founded on principles which its supporters call highminded and its critics merely fanatical. That the former are fully dedicated is not in doubt. But how, in practice, are 'total involvement' and 'total acceptance' interpreted in the day-to-day affairs of a school in which parents, children and teachers (in that order) have an equal say?

As things are, the Free School's curriculum, if it can be called that, leaves itself open to the charge of being more therapeutic than educational. Drifting in and out as the spirit moves them, the children's approach to learning tends to amount to little more than splashing about with poster paints interspersed with occasional visits to places of interest like Chester Zoo. As an attempt to exploit the resources for learning in a great city, the Scotland Road experiment cannot hold a candle to the Parkway Program (Philadelphia's 'school without walls'). How could it, after all?

Some of its pupils are so disenchanted with education as to be completely uncontrollable, the kind who refuse pointblank to comply with compulsory attendance regulations. For *them*, if for no one else, the 'come and go as you please' atmosphere of a centre which keeps open house, where play is work and work is 'just living' may have its attractions. For the rejects of the education system there is something to be said for it, if only as a place to come in from the cold. Total acceptance may be a tall order, but how else is the dropout's deeprooted fear of failure to be removed? When the greatest of all problems is to persuade hostile teenagers to set foot inside a school of any sort formal studies are best kept hidden beneath a welcome-mat.

It is claimed that all the pupils can read and write, and presumably as time goes on more attention will be paid to this side of the work. Not surprisingly no one has asked the Trust to make good its offer to provide courses for GCE candidates, which is perhaps as well seeing that at present it would find it next to impossible. Quite apart from the daily and weekly worries of trying to make ends meet, the Free School has more pressing problems to contend with. If its activities seem to be largely unstructured, at times even pointless, it is because the immediate aim is to foster a sense of belonging – the Liverpudlian version of Dewey's shared experience – without which any attempt at formal instruction would be a mockery.

Like squatters who have been served with an eviction order, these good companions are cheered by the conviction that theirs is a just cause. Freedom fighters or misguided rebels? Only the hasty-minded will wish to pronounce judgement one way or the other. As an experiment, the Scotland Road Free School has all too few prospects of surviving. Nevertheless, it has blazed a trail for others to follow. While it would be untrue to say that the free school movement is spreading like wildfire, there are plans afoot, or rumours of plans, for similar ventures in London, Manchester, Edinburgh and other cities. Given anything like the inducements offered in Denmark – indeed, given half a chance and a hint of encouragement – there is little doubt that this underground movement would surface in a big way. Anyone who wishes to fathom the motivation behind the 'idea' of the free school might do worse than read the inscription at the foot of the Statue of Liberty. That monument, it will be recalled, was erected to salute refugees who had turned their backs for ever on the Old World.

> Give me your tired, your poor,
> Your huddled masses yearning to breathe free,
> The wretched refuse of your teeming shore.
> Send these, the homeless, tempest-tost to me.

4 Day release into life release

To say that most learning occurs outside the classroom is to state the obvious – rather like saying that there are many more species in the animal kingdom than are to be found in zoo cages. And if we cannot bring ourselves to agree with Dewey that learning is all one with living, the historical record should remind us that throughout the ages there have been many examples of educational institutions which functioned *al fresco*. No apologies are needed, therefore, for introducing the concept of a school without walls without surrounding it in quotation marks. If extra-mural courses have come to be seen as a 'respectable' extension of university teaching, and if extracurricular activities are now looked upon as desirable, not to say a *sine qua non*, in secondary schools, it needs no feat of imagination to envisage a school organization which carries this outward-looking approach to its logical conclusion. As it is, most schools arrange for occasional field trips, holiday camps and visits to places of interest, and many teachers would agree that the work involved in these is as much a part of their duties as the giving of formal instruction.

A school without walls represents a systematic attempt to give greater cohesion to these arrangements. It may be defined as a community of learners who are not confined to a particular meeting-place and whose resources for learning are drawn from the neighbourhood. More simply, in so far as they use the school premises at all, it is as a base for exploration.

The first school without walls to attract worldwide interest and attention is, of course, the Parkway Program. The project takes its name from the Benjamin Franklin Parkway, a spacious boulevard stretching from Philadelphia's City Hall to the Museum of Art and lined on either side with offices, theatres, hospitals, research institutes, laboratories, parks, libraries, television and radio stations – a concentration of commercial, technological and cultural interests unrivalled in any other American metropolitan centre. In 1969 this was the setting for an experiment in the management of resources which makes all the others seem timid and ineffectual by comparison, an experiment which is currently being replicated in a number of North American cities – Chicago, Manhattan, Rochester, Hartford, Toronto and Kansas City among others. Its first director was an Englishman, John Bremer, a classicist who taught in Leicestershire before emigrating to the USA. 'If people aren't responsible for their lives you're keeping them children,' he argued, 'Without responsibility there's no education at all. My job is to set the limits in which the operation takes place.'

The project was given its trial run in the spring of 1969 with an intake of 143 students and became fully operational during the 1969–70 school year with 500, all volunteers.* Students were not selected according to any criteria of academic ability: admission was decided by a public lottery. Between them, they represented a cross-section of the high-school population in the metropolitan area, as did the staff who asked to be seconded in order to participate in the scheme.

The headquarters of the Parkway Program are housed in an old building near the City Hall which is used mainly for administrative, social and recreational purposes. Its real 'campus' is the city of Philadelphia itself.

Students are organized in what can only be described as a loose confederation. The nucleus of this learning community is a tutorial

* The 1972 enrolment is 800.

group consisting of 15–18 students, a teacher and a university intern, which meets four times a week to discuss its plans and report progress. A collection of these groups forms a 'unit' of some 150–180 students, each working independently under its own staff and having its own headquarters. In addition, the entire student body assembles once a week – the 'town meeting'. It elects or appoints various management groups which are responsible for such activities as fund-raising, organizing social functions, publishing a news-sheet and printing course catalogues. It is an integral part of the plan that as much as possible of the administrative routine should devolve on to the students themselves.

The catalogue of courses – no fewer than eighteen are listed under mathematics alone – ranges from Zen water-colours and candlemaking to Hebrew and Plato's *Dialogues*. Since all students must satisfy the requirements of the Pennsylvania State Board of Education which specifies minimum standards of attainment in English, mathematics, social studies and general science for the award of a high-school diploma, some of these courses are classed as 'faculty offerings'. Besides being responsible for guidance and supervision, the teacher in charge of each tutorial group has to make sure that its members do not neglect the basic skills or become so absorbed in their specialist interests that they fall below the standards of general education normally required in the senior high school. Apart from this, students are allowed to make their own choices and to go their own way.

Other courses are classed as 'institutional offerings', the difference being that the responsibility for teaching and supervision is largely delegated to one of the many institutions, agencies and organizations which have agreed to co-operate. Thus, the Philadelphia Zoo offers a course on zoology, the Franklin Institute a course on physics, the Museum of Art a course on the history of painting, *The Philadelphia Bulletin and Inquirer* a course on journalism, the District Attorney's Office and the Police Department a course on law enforcement, a big drug-manufacturing firm a course on 'The modern organization', the Insurance Company of North America a course on statistics ('What's the risk?'), the Philadelphia chapter of the American Civil Liberties Union a course on 'Law and civil rights' and so on. Students are encouraged to take at least one of these. They are also encouraged to take part-time, paid jobs and to play an active part in the affairs of the host institution wherever possible: those who opt for the 'Law and civil rights' course, for example, are expected to help in investigating complaints and preparing cases, besides attending court hearings. There are no 'grades': evaluation is on a straight pass/fail basis.

A student's typical day might include a course in journalism at the Philadelphia *Bulletin* taught by the newspaper's staff, a lecture in physical science at the Franklin Institute, lunch in a nearby coffee shop, tutorial in the Museum of Art (these groups of eighteen or so, which meet four times a week, are the base, something like a family, in which students receive counselling, instruction in the basic skills and evaluation), and a couple of hours' work in a downtown auto shop or a furniture-maker's studio in the little Bohemia of Sansom Street. Parkway students can conceivably spend the morning in an office building a few blocks from the Delaware River, Philadelphia's eastern boundary, and the afternoon at the University of Pennsylvania, forty blocks westward. Obviously, the Parkway Program involves a good deal of walking, but students who need to travel more than ten blocks receive free tokens for buses and subways.

As has happened in the case of John Adams High School, Portland, the Parkway plan has given rise to a violent conflict of opinion. Hailed as an entirely new concept of secondary education, 'the ultimate high school', it has also been denounced as organized anarchy – 'a place for weirdos'. Of the volunteers who tried it during the first year not a few soon began to feel lost and asked to be transferred back to their old schools. Those who persevered tended to be equally divided between enthusiasm and disillusion. Silberman quotes the comments of a 16-year-old boy:

It's the way I think a school should be. You don't come from 9 to 3 and sit there and listen to the teacher blah, blah, blah, put the answers down on the test sheet, get up and walk out and forget it. Here it's made interesting enough for you to want to know. On the bad-weather days I fought my mother to come; she'd say, 'You're not going to school today', and I'd get up and walk out – whereas I had the worst attendance record on record at the old school; I was absent 112 days last year.

Against this, a former Parkway student is quoted as saying, 'It was good experience but I wasn't really getting anything out of it. All I really learned about was people. My other school is a memorizing game – I know that – but the Parkway Program's not what I want. I learned a lot about myself but I didn't learn the things I'll need for college.'

Both attitudes are perfectly understandable. Even allowing for cross-cultural differences, it seems certain that they would be duplicated, and for the same reasons, if a similar scheme were to be operated in Britain. On his own admission, the first boy is a near dropout who feels that he has nothing to lose by absenting himself from a conventional secondary school, a born rebel who is exhilarated by his new-found freedom. The second boy's assessment of the situation is the more revealing; a frank, if fatalistic acknowledgement of the pressures of conformity and the social and economic sanctions invoked against those who resist them. What he is saying, in effect, is 'That's the way it is: you can't beat the system. Going to school may be a pretty pointless game, but anyone who refuses to play ball is sure to be penalized. Learning about people, learning about oneself, learning to find one's way around and stand on one's own feet – none of these earns "credit" for college entrance or the world of work; and until they do there is nothing for it but to toe the line like everyone else. The risks are too great, except perhaps for the mug, the martyr or the odd man out.'

He has a point. Bremer's ideal of 'people without walls' may be lofty, but as one of his associates observes, there are reasons for fearing that American society may not be ready for the kind of people that Parkway students are preparing to become.* Silberman, likewise, after paying tribute to the serious-mindedness and intellectual excitement generated by the experiment in its early stages, ends his otherwise appreciative account of it by wondering what will happen if a substantial proportion of Philadelphia high-school students decide that this is the way to get their education. To date, the institutions offering their services have not been called upon to accommodate more than a handful: conceivably, their goodwill might soon be exhausted if they were asked to accommodate students *en masse*. As noted previously, pressure of numbers caused the breakdown of the Khruschev 'Life and work'

* Dr Bremer left the Program in September 1970.

reforms in Soviet schools after 1958, and a similar breakdown may well be anticipated in the event of a wholesale participation by the older age-groups of the secondary school population. Sceptics may also be left wondering whether the wealth of resources within easy walking distance in downtown Philadelphia can be matched in other cities, let alone in the small town or the rural district.

The first of these implied criticisms – that so loosely structured an educational process is bound to produce social misfits – is only too familiar. It has been levelled against progressive theory and practice from the beginning, and there is no denying that it has force. Whether it be Parkway, Playway or Summerhill, any policy which allows the learner to fend for himself must expect to be charged with being blindly irresponsible.

The more daring the innovation, the greater the certainty of its incurring disapproval. It overcomes opposition and gains support gradually, if at all, by infiltrating the established order. In a stable, orthodox society this may not always be possible. Even in the relatively unstable, changing conditions of contemporary American society, Bremer's libertarianism, like Neill's in England, tends to be seen as potentially subversive, granting autonomy to the learner without any of the precautions usually thought necessary to secure his socialization. Yet at the same time, curiously enough, this suspicion of the innovator is tinged with admiration for his sheer effrontery. How else to explain the glare of publicity which has been focussed on so essentially modest an enterprise as the Parkway Program. As more and more schools follow its lead, the chances are that modes of self-discipline at present dismissed as merely undisciplined, and methods of organization which are apparently disorganized, will be seen as more in keeping with the temper of modern youth than the ones they seek to replace. Without necessarily counting on the emergence of a counter-culture (a more distant eventuality in Britain than it is in parts of the USA) we may see the right to be different increasingly asserted.

As for the fear that the problems involved in the release of large numbers of adolescents from compulsory school attendance will eventually prove to be insuperable, there is no immediate cause for alarm: clearing the first few fences is going to be difficult enough without worrying too much about finishing the course. If the Parkway Program has done nothing more, it has demon-strated that an alternative to secondary schooling *is* feasible. For a long time to come, fairly clearly, it is not going to be possible to organize schools without walls for more than a minority. As things are, the most workable arrangements will almost certainly not appeal to the academically inclined, neither will they suit the backward or feckless pupil incapable of making good use of the opportunities offered. On the other hand, release under proper supervision might well meet with a ready response from many 14–16-year-olds who are not enrolled for any kind of leaving-certificate course. Just what that response might be, what safeguards would be necessary, what selection procedures would have to be devised in order to satisfy the authorities and, not least, what is meant by 'proper supervision' – all these must remain in doubt until they are put to the test. In view of the general bankruptcy of ideas about what to do with 'the extra year', the raising of the school-leaving age presents Britain with the chance, indeed the challenge, for a controlled experiment in curriculum development which should not be missed. Such an experiment might, or might not, be modelled on the Philadelphia prototype. It has to be remembered that the organization of British secondary schools, particularly those which answer to the description of open schools, is, on the whole, less repressive than that of many American high schools, that social malaise is nothing like so rife here as it has been in recent years on the other side of the Atlantic, and that the age-groups likely to be involved are slightly younger.

There remains the objection that Philadelphia is a special case and that what has been done there is unlikely to be repeated with anything like the same success elsewhere. This is defeatist. Anyone who has doubts on this score need only follow the advice of his local telephone directory, 'Save your legs. Ring round with Yellow Pages'.

A glance through the classified trades and professions in the Glasgow and district directory, for example, quickly reveals a lengthy ABC of possible sources of recruitment:

Accountants
Advertising agencies
Airport
Architects
Art galleries and museums service
Associations – social, cultural and general
Auctioneers

Automobile Association
Bakers and confectioners
Banks
Booksellers
Brewers and bottlers
Brickmakers
British Broadcasting Corporation
British Railways
Builders and contractors
Bus and coach services
Butchers
Car distributors and dealers
Careers Advisory Service
Catering trades
Cattle breeders and dealers
Charitable and benevolent organizations
Chemical manufacturers and suppliers
Churches
Civil engineering
Clinics
Clubs – social and general
Collieries
Computers
Co-operative societies
Courts

– enough to be going on with, it may be thought.

For the sake of argument, seeing that *someone* has to initiate it, let us suppose that an enterprising head teacher of a comprehensive school draws up a complete list of local institutions, organizations and agencies whose co-operation might, in his opinion, be desirable. Having done this, his next step is to find out what prospects there are, if any, of enlisting this co-operation. With this in mind he makes a few preliminary inquiries. Needless to say, this calls for discretion, for as yet he is in no position to issue a declaration of intent and can only put out vague feelers. Most of this sounding out will be done best through personal contacts (it will help enormously if this head teacher of ours is a prominent Rotarian!).

Accordingly, Mr X, our head teacher, seeks an interview with his director of education. He explains to him that the underlying purpose of the scheme is not to provide pre-vocational training but rather to enhance the general education of older pupils who, for one reason or other, seem to have reached a dead end so far as classroom instruction is concerned. He points out, however, that many young people change jobs half a dozen times during the first eighteen months after leaving school. Under a release scheme they might 'shop around', so to speak, and gain more from first-hand experience in a wide range of occupational and social settings than they could from formal studies. The ones who stand to benefit most, in his view, are the so-called Newsom children – *not* the 'Robinson' boys and girls, he hastens to add, nor the 'Browns', but the middle-of-the-road 'Joneses'. These are the ones whose interest often flags and whose motivation nosedives during the last two years of compulsory school attendance. Ultimately, he would like to see the 'Robinsons' given their chance, but he is enough of a realist to see that the inclusion of an unruly element might bring discredit on the experiment from the start, and probably cause its early abandonment.

As regards selection, he would limit the catchment to 14–16-year-olds who were reasonably proficient in the basic subjects but who showed signs of apathy, boredom, a sense of marking time or just going through the motions of schoolbound learning.

After thinking over the proposal, the director decides that the best course is to hand it over to a small committee consisting of three headmasters, a guidance expert, an administrative assistant and an educational psychologist whose task will be to carry out a feasibility study.

The committee forthwith sets about its business as a team. The guidance expert and the educational psychologist interview children with the appropriate scholastic records to find out which of them are able and willing to be registered as external students. (The suggestion is that they should be designated as 'registered external students' and carry an identity card to that effect as proof of their *bona fides* when not attending school.) The headmasters hold staff meetings and meetings with parents to explain the reasons for wishing to launch the scheme and how it is likely to operate in practice. The administrative assistant writes round Mr X's list of probables asking whether they are prepared to accept registered external students and, if so, under what conditions. It is made clear that, to begin with, the numbers involved will be small – probably not more than 40 all told. A provisional time-table is eventually worked out and a provisional list of names is drawn up.

The committee reports back to the director seeking his per-mission for a pilot run during the spring term, a sort of sandwich course to be followed by a return to school after Easter. A principal guidance teacher and one of his assistants have agreed to act as supervisors, but it is hoped that it will not be necessary to ask for their secondment from their normal duties – the idea is that their role will be rather like that of college of education lecturers keeping an eye on students during their periods of teaching practice. Before being sent out, registered external students will need to be thoroughly briefed, but in general the success or failure of the experiment will depend upon what they do for themselves rather than upon what their supervisors do for them. If they abuse the trust placed in them, e.g. by making a nuisance of them-selves in the host organization, steps will be taken to ensure their immediate withdrawal from the scheme. It should be emphasized, however, that any evaluation of success will need to be done more in terms of affective and attitudinal changes than in terms of cognitive gains, and that a single term may not be long enough for any significant changes of this kind to be detectable. The educational psychologist already has profiles of the children who have been selected and it is hoped that the correlation between these and scores on the relevant tests which will be administered on return to school will afford some measure of the effects of block release. A control group of children whose profiles are essentially similar to those of the registered external students will remain in full-time school attendance. If permission is given, the written consent of the parents will be necessary.

The feasibility study is approved and the committee given a cautious go-ahead. What happens thereafter is best recounted in the pages of a 15-year-old's imaginary diary:

Weeks 1 and 2 – Central Hotel. Posh place, people coming and going all the time. Manager showed Jimmy and me around first morning, after which we were left on our own. Receptionist seems to think we're unofficial pageboys. Mr Z looked in to see how we were getting on. Told him not so bad. First week OK, second a dead loss.

Week 3 – *Zoo*. Fantastic! Spent the first day going the rounds with the head keeper. Liked him a lot – until he got the two of us to help clean out the elephant house. Some people! 6″ of snow on Wednesday, freezing hard. Wish I was back at the Central Hotel. Not cut out for out-of-doors life. Even the animals look miserable.

Weeks 4 *and* 5 – *Car distributors and garage*. What a dump! Seem to be in everybody's way. On my own, too – Jimmy's off with the flu (all that snow last week). Glad when Mr Z dropped in for a talk: he left me a list of things to look out for. Have learned the names of all the latest models in the showroom, mileages of used cars, list prices, etc. – in other words damn all. Most of the time in the repair shop. Foreman treats me as if I were an unpaid mechanic's mate, expects me to lend a hand at the filling station. The elephant house was better than this.

Week 6 – *Marks and Spencer's*. Wouldn't mind being a house detective – feel rather like one myself except when I'm kept busy unpacking crates etc. in the storeroom. Expected to stay until closing time which means getting home late in the evening.

Week 7 – *Automobile Association*. First two days at Fanum House. Found the Emergency Breakdown Service most interesting. Wednesday and Thursday out in patrol car.

Weeks 8–9 – *Museum and Art Gallery*. Director spent quite a bit of time showing us round the exhibits. Listened to three lectures on the French Impressionists – notebook full of names but the natural history section is more in my line. Worked with the curator in the taxidermy room.

Week 10 – *Central Station*. If only it had been the airport!

Weeks 11–12 – *St. Thomas's Church Hall*. Wasn't looking forward to this one but it's surprising how much parsons have to do, visiting old people, hospitals, even prisons. Rev. A really took Jimmy and me under his wing, made us feel we weren't just kids.

There we must leave it. What happens when these 40 registered external students return to their classrooms for the last time is anybody's guess. If it turns out that the research findings report no significant differences, as they frequently do, the experiment may be written off as a failure, in which case the chances are that it will be discontinued. It may be that the consensus of opinion will be

G

that the whole thing has been a waste of time, or even that the experience has left some 15-year-olds feeling that they would much rather be in school. Alternatively, the outcome might be the breakthrough for which the educational world is waiting.

'This, Sir, was the commencement of the plan', as Robert Raikes wrote in 1783, a plan conceived, as his was, in the belief that 'it would be at least a harmless attempt, if it were productive of no good'. For all they know, Mr X and his director may have made the first moves in a continuous process which began in the nineteenth century by herding adolescents willy-nilly into schools and ends, if not today then tomorrow or the day after, by returning them to their rightful place in society.

APPENDIXES

Appendix 1

The Resources Centre, Codsall Comprehensive School, Staffs.

How to order work through the Resources Centre

To prevent waste, both in terms of money and time, please check to see that the item you are intending to produce is not already in the Centre, and that you are producing the item in the most economic way.

All orders through the Resources Centre must be accompanied by an instruction slip. (Pink). Please tick the necessary sections and leave your item in the respective trays in the Reprographic Room. *If you require your item to be permanently stored you must also complete a feature slip for each item.*

To guarantee good service, plan ahead, and give the Centre staff as much time as possible to produce your teaching material.

Under normal circumstances work will be done in the order in which it is received.

Completed items will be left in the staff Workshop. Material will be cleared away every Friday and stored in the Resources Centre.

Audio-visual

The following equipment is available through the Resources Centre:

Cameras: 2 Voigtlander 35 mm
1 Praktica Nova 1B (Reflex) 35 mm with meter and Domiplan lens
1 set of extension tubes for above
Hacker record player GP/42 Mod.
Coomba record player GSP/25/12W
Kodak Carousel S. Projector
150 mm I.S.C.O. lens
100 mm   ,,   ,,
Case for carrying above
Phillips Cassette – model N 2202
Photax 401 hand viewer
Photax Solar hand viewer
Microphones
Hand/Stand
8 mm camera and projector
Hannimex Hanorama hand viewer
Hannimex 2000 syllabus and slide and filmstrip carrier
Hannimette slide and filmstrip projector
Graflex filmstrip viewer
Gnome 8″ × 8″ rear projection screen
  ,,   12″ × 12″ ,,   ,,   ,,
  ,,   18″ × 18″ ,,   ,,   ,,
50″ × 50″ Argenta tripod daylight screen
2 Tandberg 1521 tape recorders
Overhead projector
Amplifiers/Speakers
Television
Epidiascope
8 mm loop projector
(2) 16 mm projectors

Appendix 2

Background Papers: John Adams High School, Portland, Oregon

The Philosophy of John Adams High School
Ratification Draft

John Adams High School believes that public education needs to change. It seeks to effect that change through providing quality education for students in a setting where training, research and evaluation are integral parts of the institution. The school strives to provide this quality education in a humane and open setting and to deal with each student's individual capacities, needs and interests. It also proposes to place a primary emphasis on teaching students *how* to learn, since the amount of knowledge in the world continues to accumulate at a rate beyond the comprehension of any individual. And finally, the school attempts to prepare students from mixed racial, social and economic backgrounds to become literate, verbal and experienced in the processes of problem-solving, so that they may exercise and create as many options as possible in the rapidly changing world of the future.

22 October 1971

The Objectives of John Adams High School

1. The school will treat each student as an individual, affirm his self-worth as a human being, and will work with him to tailor an educational programme, that will fit his present and future needs and interests.
2. The school will organize a variety of programmes which will increase each student's skills in reading, writing, listening, speech, computation, critical and creative thinking and physical development.
3. The school will provide educational activities which aim at the discovery of what is true, and which stress the interrelatedness of form and content in knowledge as well as the interrelatedness of the various areas of knowledge.
4. The school will provide opportunities for students to develop their capacity for making choices and will confront students with the need to take responsibility for their own educational experiences and for their actions within the school setting.
5. The school will provide a setting where each member of the school community understands and acts in accordance with democratic principles, and participates in the making of decisions which affect him.
6. The school will provide a setting which allows a student to experience and explore a wide range of human relationships in order for him to learn about himself and how to live compatibly with a variety of life styles and manners.
7. The school will provide experiences for the student which will help him both in the selection of a career and in understanding the place and value of leisure.
8. The school will provide a system of surveying and making arrangements within the community so that the human and physical resources of the school and the community can be mutually shared.
9. The school will combine in one institution a comprehensive urban high school, a site for on-the-job training of staff, and a site for research into and evaluation of the effects of this institution on reform in public education.

General Education: Guiding Principles

General Education is a course of study which students at John Adams take in lieu of the minimally required courses in English, social studies, general mathematics and basic science. It is cross-disciplinary in that it synthesizes information and uses modes of analysis from different disciplines. The twofold purpose is to help students develop a sense of competence as an individual and as a member of a group. General Education proposes to teach young people to learn how to learn by incorporating a variety of programmes – such as the Education Professions Development Act, Title I – to establish positive self-images, to identify and remedy skill deficiencies, to define research questions, to gather and analyse data, and to develop skills in organizing and communicating the appropriate findings. Students who have completed General Education will have gained extensive individual and group experiences in studying issues and problems and in developing strategies for acting upon those that face all of us in the world today. Teachers are brought from different academic backgrounds on to teams that jointly plan and teach in ways that help students find their balance between conflicting views, particularly as the students frequently study problems in as realistic a manner as possible in the community outside the walls of the school.

General Education: Team Management and Team Teaching Objectives

1. Each team will fashion a philosophy of team operation which includes a commitment to the General Education programme and the co-operative decision-making process of the team.
2. Each team will provide an atmosphere so that all team members will work through common problems – curriculum, instruction, training, management, evaluation – together.
3. Each team will formulate an academic programme for each school year.
4. Each team staff member will treat all students on the team as a part of that team:
   a. Every adult on the team is a teacher to all the students on the team.
   b. Team staff members know and have a voice in what happens to all students.

   c. Team will offer time to consult with students, teachers, counsellors, parents and support other people when necessary.

5. Each team will establish an accurate and comprehensive system of record-keeping including:
   a. attendance reporting
   b. academic credit and grades
   c. possible test data
   d. other team activities, such as field trips.

6. Each team, under the leadership of the Team Leader, will assume responsibility for implementing district policies and procedures as outlined in the Faculty Handbook.

8. Each team will compile, in a transferable manner, curriculum materials and suggested procedures, for the information of other teams.

General Education: Instructional Objectives

1. The student will improve his skills in writing, speaking, listening, reading and reasoning by:
   a. recognizing differing forms of literary and oral expression and using a variety of language styles in a society which demands that standard forms be used for political and economic survival.
   b. showing improvement in identifying his own communication skills which need development.
   c. showing improvement in written communication, especially in the area of spelling and vocabulary, punctuation and sentence structure and overall conceptual clarity.
   d. demonstrating through frequent analysis – written and verbal – comprehension of assigned reading, listening and visual materials.
   e. demonstrating the ability to evaluate ideas and concepts, methods and materials, by using criteria appropriate to the medium being evaluated.
   f. showing improvement in articulating his interpretation of ideas and events to others and to comprehend and evaluate others' interpretations.

2. The student will demonstrate the ability to use the process of problem analysis and decision-making by:

    a. using the sequence of observation – description – analysis – verification – solution – in dealing with important problems and issues, not only in the classroom but beyond to contemporary problems in his life and community.

    b. constructing and participating in fair procedures to conduct group decision-making.

    c. protecting individual, minority and majority rights.

3. The student will experience the interrelatedness of knowledge. The student will demonstrate an understanding of the uses of knowledge by:

    a. formulating and participating in study projects and activities that cut across traditional subject-matter categories.

    b. using data and materials from many traditional subject-matter categories when analysing problems.

    c. stating the underlying assumptions, special interest, attitudes, and perspectives of various individuals or groups involved in the same complex situation.

    d. applying previously learned facts, concepts, methods, in new situations.

4. The student will question and take action on the things which affect his life – people, processes and institutions – by:

    a. comprehending own needs and defining these to others.

    b. comprehending the structured relationships that affect his life: work, school, home, etc.

    c. questioning other individuals' arguments, needs and expectations.

    d. understanding the different interpretations given to such concepts as 'democracy' and 'participation' and be able to formulate, explain and advocate his own interpretation of confusing concepts.

5. The student's affective development will be enhanced through the General Education team by:

    a. seeking out a variety of appropriate ways to experience success.

    b. accepting differences in other people.

    c. gaining confidence and respect for himself.

    d. feeling competent in pursuing his given set of goals.

    e. discovering how to effect changes in himself.

f. feeling a sense of belonging to the team.

g. feeling useful in team activities.

h. attending class regularly and accounting for absences.

Letter from Donald D. Holt, Principal of John Adams High School

We have begun to move away from the original design and intention of General Education. Perhaps it is more accurate to say we have begun to expand the rather narrow design of the original GenEd programme. As a curriculum model it was, and still is, a bold and exciting venture. As an applicable entity for use in an inner-city school it has shown some considerable drawbacks. For one thing, it did not sufficiently attack the problem of basic skill deficiency so apparent in a large number of our students. It presupposed a level of inquiry that our students did not or could not generate. As a curriculum model it lacked the necessary operational components to respond to the diverse needs of our students. For us, the delivery system for any curriculum package is a critical variable. As one writer recently put it, the concern should be for new settings within which we face each other, and new arrangements that encourage the qualities regarded as important by all the participants. General Education had been taught in a daily one-hour time block. The focus, consequently, had to be a heavily subject-matter one. Considering our staff and philosophy, that amount of time was not sufficient to show a positive intrusion into many lives. Additionally, we discovered that we had not adequately reduced the impact of a large sprawling institution and all it signals to students.

In an attempt to continue our quest for personalization of the schooling at John Adams, we are now deeply involved in the creation of smaller schools within the larger institution. In broad terms, it could be considered analogous to our original house design. We discovered that 400 students were just too many to deal with. We are now attempting to reduce the 'agency' size to 150 students. Our ultimate goal is to have approximately seven schools, as autonomous as possible, surrounded by the support services they need, and operating either within our building or outside, depending on available facilities. It is still in a crude form, but next year we will have one team of students and teachers (150 students, five teachers, one counsellor, and one intern) functioning as a school-within-a-school. Five more teams will be working on a half-day basis with students. We are intentionally going slowly. We learned the first year that the complete leap is dangerous and unmanageable.

About the senate: we did start with a student and faculty senate. They didn't last long. We found the theory of participatory democracy ran headlong into battles over control. We simply substituted one power base for another (staff for administration), and the result was politicalization that had little to do with education. The obvious conclusion one could draw from all this would be that it should have been a marvellous learning experience for students. To be in such an exciting environment must surely have provided students models from which to engage in stimulating dialogue about government and all that it means. It didn't happen that way. The adults squeezed the students out, made their battles the key encounters, and left the students to shuffle for themselves. They shuffled for a short time and then said 'to hell with it'. We are now all working together to pick up the pieces.

It is my opinion that in spite of the administrative changes that have taken place at John Adams, we are still continuing our quest for the identification of something that makes sense in urban education. The things we take for granted in our current programme, schools around this country are still debating. Ungraded curriculum, pass-fail evaluation, the completely elective curriculum, programme design by students, a clinical training site for student teachers, interns, social workers, aides, and para-professionals and research-based decision-making are all given at John Adams. As yet, these are not enough.

Appendix 3

Schools without walls:
Rochester N.Y. and Watertown, Mass.

The School Without Walls: Rochester N.Y.

For the programme to work we need people who are willing to devote a small portion of their time to assisting interested young people who want to work in, explore, or observe the real functioning of their community. In a sense we are trying to enable our students to participate in, or at least to observe, all aspects of their environment at work in much the same way that the small town youth of the nineteenth century could see his world. Let them see what you do, help in your operations, and ask you questions.

Let them see what your work world is like – its problems as well as its pleasures. The natural result of many such exposures can only be students who are capable of understanding the operation of their world as it really is, rather than as something mysterious, controlled by insensitive, unresponsive, mythic monsters. They then are in a far better position to make reasoned choices about their own futures.

Basically the most important asset that you can offer to our students is yourself. You are out there where things are really being done. Where in many ways you are helping to shape the world we all live in. What could be more important to young people facing choices that will determine the direction of their lives than our awareness of both the satisfactions and the very real frustrations that each of us confronts daily? Only by seeing and participating in your real world can they come to understand what you have already learned (mostly by direct experience yourself): that life is a compound of these satisfactions *and* frustrations.

The operational idea here is *resource*. Let them or help them to frame a problem or series of questions that you can answer, and work with them to find some of the possible answers. In many cases you will be more successful if you follow *their* concerns than if you try to carefully structure a presentation that gets across what *you* feel they should know. Let your answers provide the food for more questions. You might not have to prepare anything in advance; your experience and your life have been your preparation. You set the time limits. The *amount* of time that you are prepared to give directly yourself is one concern. The amount of time you are willing to allow a student to involve *himself* is another. You also establish total duration of involvement: two weeks, a month, ten weeks – that's up to you. The staff of the School Without Walls will work with you and the students to help clarify directions and define reachable goals.

Share with us the faith that what school and society have been *saying* is essential to an education is really important. But let the student *find* these essentials himself.

Our students, like us, best learn what interests them or what they see as necessary. The School Without Walls lets the student's interests and initiative become the motivation for his learning.

You are not being asked to do *our* job or to be a buddy, pal, or 'big brother' to these students. Just make yourself available to share your valuable experience and knowledge on your own terms with interested students. In this way, you can provide more than classroom teachers and textbooks can: *The taste of reality.*

History of the Home Base School
INCEPTION
Spring & Summer, 1970

The need for an alternative high school was expressed by the
Watertown community during the Watertown Charrette in May,
1970. The Charrette was a federally-funded week-long planning
session open to all members of the Town and was the culmination
of several months of study by committees of citizens concerned
with such areas as taxes, education, recreation and government.
The participants of the Charrette agreed on the following assump-
tions about education:

1. That those who must live with decisions should play an active
   role in making them.
2. That people can learn in many places outside school buildings.
3. That the Greater Boston Community had many resources which
   could be tapped and
4. That the school should involve members of the community as
   much as possible, and proposed to the Watertown School
   system the establishment of a small alternative high school of
   100 student volunteers and 6 staff in facilities outside the
   existing secondary schools.

Action on the proposal came in July. At its meeting the School
Committee, in co-operation with the Superintendent of Schools,
appointed a Watertown resident who had been active in the
Charrette Process, as a part-time administrative assistant to
co-ordinate a feasibility study of the school. The balance of the
summer was spent identifying the following as major concerns:

1. How many students were interested in the idea? How would
   they be selected?
2. How many of their parents would give permission?
3. Were there other schools like the one proposed? If so, what
   were they like?
4. Would students in such a programme be accepted in college?
5. Were there community resource people interested in working
   with the students in such a programme?
6. Could such a programme be adequately staffed?

Appendixes

201

7. What would it cost?
8. What might some student programmes look like?

DEVELOPMENT
School Year 1970–1

The first steps involved compiling data in answer to the questions. Community members who had participated in the Charrette co-operated in completing the study, and a final proposal was presented to the School Committee in November. The School Committee approved the proposal in December; after budget considerations were worked out, the School proposal contained the following elements:

1. Six staff certified at the secondary level, one in each of the following areas:
   Guidance Counselling
   Humanities/Arts
   Language Arts
   Mathematics/Sciences
   Social Sciences
   Technical/Vocational
2. One of the staff members would serve as a co-ordinator of the team.
3. 100 students, 25 in each of grades 9–12, selected at random from volunteers having written parental permission.
4. Facilities located out of the existing secondary building.
5. A full-time secretary
6. Car and driver to facilitate travel to field experiences.
7. Money for bus and subway fares to facilitate travel to field experiences.
8. Release time for staff planning in Spring, 1971.
9. Two weeks of summer planning time for the staff.

The Town also applied and received approval for funds under Title III of the Federal Elementary and Secondary Education Act, for innovative projects, to supplement the planning money and to develop an evaluation design appropriate for this unique kind of school.

Upon approval of the Home Base School budget, six staff members were selected whose qualifications included certification in one of the above six areas and team leadership ability. Staff selection was completed by March with five of the six positions being filled by people from the Watertown Schools.

During the Spring the new staff began meeting weekly to plan for the school. It was strongly believed that almost all final decisions regarding structure of the school and its curriculum should be held until students had been selected and consulted. At this time the staff members informed every eligible student about the Home Base School through visitations to all English classes in the 8th–11th grades. Interested students were given information for their parents and a parental permission form. Meanwhile evening meetings were held for parents who desired more information before deciding. There were more than 200 applicants from which 100 were selected by drawing names from a hat, 25 students per grade. The remainder were placed on a waiting list in the order in which they were drawn.

Thus the school community was complete, and the long process of working out exactly what the school would be began. A series of large and small group meetings were held with students, parents and staff to clarify goals and needs for all involved in the Home Base School.

In late Spring, members of the Home Base School staff began discussing with members of the faculty of the new Graduate Programme in Open Education at Newton College of the Sacred Heart to explore possibilities of collaboration between the programmes.

Summer, 1971

A formal three week summer workshop was held to design the basic structure of the school – two of these weeks included as many students as could be there. The issues addressed included the following: (1) new roles and responsibilities, (2) the design of courses, (3) the planning of individual programmes, (4) the identification of resource people and places and (5) the decision-making process to be used in the school. The staff portion of this workshop was used to develop an outline of an evaluation design; consultant help was utilized in this process.

It was decided to form a Community Advisory Committee to

facilitate interaction between and among the various constituencies of the Home Base School. Membership included members of the School Department, parents, students and community resources. In addition to including a representative student, parent and staff member from the school, efforts were made to involve people not otherwise connected with the Home Base School.

The original discussion with the Newton College Graduate Programme resulted in a summer Planning Grant from the New England Programme in Teacher Education. As finally developed, the project called for hiring four Newton College graduate students as interns on the Home Base School staff with specific responsibilities to facilitate the sharing of resources among the Home Base School, the Newton College Graduate Programme and the people of the Watertown Community. The interns were also to work closely with resource people to help make their experiences as resources of maximum value to both themselves and the students. The proposal was developed by faculty and staff at both the Home Base School and Newton College and by the four graduate students subsequently appointed as interns. At the end of the summer the project was funded and the interns were appointed. In addition to teaching some courses, each intern had a series of tasks specifically related to the project, among them: (1) the establishment of a data bank of resource people (2) arranging visitations, (3) scheduling and running meetings of resource people and (4) responding to mailed inquiries about the Home Base School.

Facilities were leased for the school year from the Saint James Armenian Youth and Cultural Centre in Watertown. The space includes one room used as a school office, one large multi-use room, one lounge and three classrooms (one of which is used primarily for music, arts and crafts).

The full-time staff included the original six staff, four graduate interns from Newton College, one secretary and one driver; part-time staff included two evaluation consultants and one administrative assistant to administer the fiscal aspects of the Title III grant and the grant from the New England Programme in Teacher Education.

THE FIRST YEAR
School Year 1971–2

The Home Base School officially opened in September 1971 with the biggest job of all ahead – putting ideas into practice. Many of the areas below will reflect the changes in the school structure that occurred in the attempts to meet the goals of the school.

Programmes – Student programmes are constructed by the students with guidance from staff members and parents. These programmes have a dual focus – inward towards the school and outward towards the community. Between the courses and programmes offered at Home Base and the field experiences and courses available in the Boston community, the needs and interests of each student can be met. It is the belief of the school that this balance between school and community is essential to the educational experience of students. Learning experiences vary from fairly normal-sounding courses like 'Algebra I' and 'Grammar and Composition' to unique programmes at the school like the experimental theatre, music theory, photography, karate, to field work at the Franklin Park Zoo, Coombs Motors, the Boston University Medical Centre and Perkins Institute for the Blind. Some of these are offered by staff, others by resource people from the community. There are more than 90 resource people listed on file; more than 60 are active currently. Students are encouraged to take at least one course outside the Home Base School. The evaluation of an individual's performance in a learning experience is expected to be a process involving both the resource for the experience and the learner. The evaluations are written and placed in a student's folder; copies are given to the students to be transmitted to their parents. In January students reorganized their programmes with staff assistance, bringing in new resource teachers and developing many new community-based experiences.

One of the important programmes offered at the school is the experimental theatre, providing several beneficial functions not foreseen in the fall. At its inception, it was meant to be a programme to offer lighting and set design, acting, directing, dance and the basics of carpentry and electricity as components to technical theatre. As the year progressed, it was found that the theatre involved many students from widely differing backgrounds and interests until approximately 50 per cent of the school was involved. For those whose energies and/or talents were artistically predisposed, for those who had no theatrical interest *per se* but found a chance to work on technical skills involved in building the control booth with its lighting and sound consoles, and for those who felt an uneasiness with their new non-structured freedom, and found some security in the self-discipline demanded in the theatre, the Home Base Experimental Theatre proved to be reasonably exciting and fairly cohesive. During its first year the company produced Shakespeare's *A Midsummer Night's Dream*, a production whose audiences included Watertown's elementary school children, *Antigone* by Sophocles, whose costumes were photographed and included in a book on design soon to be published in New York, and *Summertree*, a contemporary anti-war play which included as a prologue a satirical revue written, choreographed, directed and costumed by the students.

School Groups – The summer workshop established a complex Town Meeting form of school government in which most discussion and voting was done in small groups – the large group being reserved for presentation of issues and for sharing small group conclusions. The decisions from this form of government were deadlocked so often that people lost interest and eventually tried a simplified version of the Town Meeting – with elected moderators, a published agenda, and discussion and voting on the floor of the large group with a majority of those present and voting sufficient to carry a decision. This method also died, since students began to feel if they weren't at the meeting to register dissent, then the decision did not apply to them. A student came up with a proposal for the present government in early Spring. It is a representative government consisting of three parents, six students and two staff. This government has agreed to terminate in December to be evaluated and reorganized if necessary. The group meets weekly to deal with issues affecting school policy.

Another outgrowth of the summer workshops was the establishment of weekly discussion groups to provide a forum for non-directed student discussion, a place to 'let off steam' in the hopes of fostering a sense of community at Home Base. These groups were co-led by a student and one of the original six staff and each contained approximately one-sixth of the students. The co-leaders met weekly in a seminar in group leadership skills run by a sociologist at a local university, the staff co-leaders receiving local in-service credit for the seminar and the student co-leaders receiving credit in the social sciences.

The parents established a Council of Home Base School parents and elected an Executive Committee that meets at least once a month with members of the staff and student body who are both interested and available. This group has sponsored some fund-raising efforts and is invaluable in getting information out to parents. They are co-ordinating efforts to reach local groups through speaking engagements at meetings, and are planning other activities involving themselves in the day-to-day operations of the school.

A review board, consisting of students, parents and staff was established to review student programmes and to establish criteria on course credits and minimum programmes.

Evaluation – Two evaluation consultants familiar with the goals of the school and experienced in evaluation methodology were hired to develop an evaluation design appropriate for the unique pro-gramme of the Home Base School and to conduct the evaluation. The emphasis of the evaluation is on both the product and the process of the school and the methodology utilizes a sociological and anthropological model rather than a systems model.

As part of their design, the evaluators developed the Intervention Team, which reported to the School areas needing immediate attention or reorganization within the school. Thus the evaluation became a tool for change during the school year rather than merely a look backward at the year's end. One of the significant changes initiated by the Intervention team was the abolition of the discussion groups established at the beginning of the year. These groups had been used for advising and keeping track of what individual students were doing as well as for non-directed student discussion. Since the groups were not a satisfactory way of meeting individual student problems and needs, and given the frequent opportunity for informal student–student and student–staff contact in the school, the Intervention team recommended discarding them. In their place the team recommended intensifying the Adviser system. Under this system each adviser is selected by ten student advisees. Each student thus receives counselling individually from the staff member he chooses. The system started slowly, but by May it was deemed of critical importance. It has helped students plan programmes objectively and has provided an outlet for their ideas and frustrations.

Planning for Next Year – Staff, students and parents participated in the selection of a new programme Chairman and new staff members for the coming school year. Prospective students were given information about the school, and random selection was used to select twenty-five new students. Graduating students were assisted in developing their future plans – all students interested in college were accepted, and most of them were admitted to the college of their first choice; students who were interested in employment have been placed in jobs in their field.

Formal procedures were developed to permit secondary school students in Watertown and other alternative schools to participate in course work at the Home Base School. Procedures were also developed to assist local universities in placing student teachers at the school. In particular, a reading programme has been arranged through Northeastern's Graduate School of Education, and practice teaching through Boston University's Foundations of Education programme.

THE SECOND YEAR
Summer, 1972

During the summer, staff have been involved in selecting evaluators for the programme, and developing a design for the evaluation. Consultants have been interviewed and criteria developed for a programme in staff development for the coming school year. A summer workshop was conducted at Newton College of the Sacred Heart as part of the Project funded by the New England Programme for Teacher Education in which the interns, Home Base staff, Newton College staff and community resource people participated.

INDEX